not home yet

HOW TO BE HUMAN IN AN INHUMAN WORLD

Brandon and Liv Booth

www.signpostinn.org

Copyright © 2024 Brandon and Liv Booth

All rights reserved.

ISBN: 979-8-9912603-0-5

DEDICATION

To every weary heart in search of a deep and abiding connection with the one true source of all things, and with deepest gratitude toward those who have welcomed us in Jesus' name.

May you know him, the Christ, Jesus.

CONTENTS

1	Not home yet	1
2	What's wrong with the world?	13
3	The first place we meet God	21
4	What gets in our way	27
5	Lies we hold onto	39
6	Who is God, really?	45
7	Pretending God is someone he's not	59
8	Learning to see God correctly	67
9	Does God want to be near me?	77
10	How?	85
11	Being vulnerable	97
12	Prayer	107
13	Church	115
14	The incarnate grace of hospitality	129
15	Hospitality as a posture	143
16	How to hospitality	149
17	How to hospitality: a guest	155
18	How to hospitality: a space	163
19	How to hospitality: a time frame	173
20	How to hospitality: a consumable	179
21	How to hospitality: a loosely-committed-to activity	187
22	Boundaries	191
23	Guesting	201
24	I needed to see it first	207

1
NOT HOME YET

Brandon

Liv and I have almost nothing in common. I am a hawk. She is a frog. I grew up on the arid plains of Colorado, a land of infinite horizons and majestic mountains. Hot winds blast towering granite perches with red dirt. And I love it.

We hawks value freedom. We crave independence. We roost high in the sunbaked cliffs and twirl on the updrafts that lift us on our majestic wings.

Liv, a frog, grew up in the swampy Northeast. For her, "home" means squishing mud between her bare toes, the smell of moss, and long days of swimming in the pond near her house. Frogs value close spaces and close relationships. They value tasty food, and above all, staying wet. Hawks do not like getting their feathers drippy.

The day after we got married, I packed my moist little frog bride into the front seat of a yellow moving van and drove her to… drumroll please… Texas. And then, after many years of sojourning all over the west, I moved her back to my home in the high desert of Colorado.

Liv has never really felt at home anywhere we've lived. The landscape has been foreign, the people strange, the expectations unclear. Since the day we got married, she has always been a frog out of water. (Literally? Figuratively? I'm not sure anymore).

As a hawk I've always loved her, but rarely understood her. So, she has often felt alone.

And here's the point. All of us feel the same way.

Dear reader, I don't know you, but there is one thing I know about you. Your life is hard. You have suffered and are suffering. You have loved and lost. You have suffered sickness and financial distress. You have been hurt, and you have hurt others. You are tired. And above all, you are lonely.

I know this because you are human. And you live in a world that doesn't feel like a home for humans.

Like frogs living in a desert, we all suffer from constant thirst. I instinctively feel there must be something more to life. More joy, more safety, more significance, more friends, more help. But those things are hard to find in a desert. I feel I should be living in a place of abundance. A place with water everywhere. But I live in a land of scarcity. My throat is always parched, my skin dry and leathery. Do you feel the same?

Some of us have tried to adapt. We've tried to find comfort or solace in the dirty pleasures of this wasteland, pretending to be lizards with hard protective scales. Some of us have tried to ignore reality. We pretend that puddles are as good as lakes or look for ways to distract ourselves from what's really going on. Others have just given up hope.

We all feel alone. Where are my froggy friends? My brothers and sisters who love to swim and play? Why is it so hard to connect? Why do I always feel like I'm the one who doesn't "get it" or that I'm the one that no one really gets?

Let me speak plainly for a moment. We humans were born in a garden. A place of abundance and life. We were meant to live in a garden city. A place with good work to do and good friends to do it with. Our deepest instincts tell us this is true. But that's not this world. At least, *not yet*.

We are all travelers in this wilderness. Sojourners in a strange land. Or, in the words of the Apostle Peter, "exiles dispersed abroad." At the same time, we are also "chosen according to the foreknowledge of God the Father, through the sanctifying work of the Spirit, to be obedient and to be sprinkled with the blood of Jesus Christ."[1]

So we are wanderers but not lost. Exiles, but not without a promised land. Lost children, but not orphans. Pilots who have crashed behind enemy lines, but the Marines are on the way.

We are homeless, but not truly without a home, we're

---

[1] 1 Peter 1:1-2 CSB

just *not home yet*.

This is the encouraging message of this book. For now, you and I are frogs out of water, *but there is water!* Real water. Abundant water. *Living* water. And our arrival there is guaranteed by the power of God the Father, the love of God the Holy Spirit, and the death and resurrection of God the Son. Even if we must suffer for a while here in this strange land, we do not need to suffer without hope!

God, my good Father, has seen my struggle and has had compassion on me. Because of his compassion he has promised to rescue me, to raise me from the dead and make me a co-heir with Christ. This world will be re-made, and I will be home. I do not need to struggle to get home. Home is finding me. It's just a matter of God's time until it gets here. Then *everywhere* will be home.

That truth changes my attitude toward life. For sure, things are hard. Some things are really hard. And some things are *unbearably hard*. I don't want to minimize or ignore just how truly horrible and awful and *evil* people and things can be in this world. Truly I don't. There are no words to describe just how bad things can get.

And yet… I do want to give even people in the worst of the worst situations hope. All evil is temporary. Whether in this life or the next it will stop and be replaced with good. (And I share the cry with so many of you, "Please, dear God, let it be in this life!") The pain will stop and be replaced with pleasure. The fear and anxiety will stop and be replaced with confidence. The loneliness will stop and be replaced with feasting and friends! Lord Jesus, come quickly!

IN THE MEANTIME

That's good news, but what about in the meantime? How do frogs live in the desert? How do humans live in an inhuman world? That's what this book is about. It's a survival guide for frogs living in a desert. An instruction manual to help you find oases full of froggy friends. It's about strengthening your relationship with Jesus and with others.

How? Well, that's a big part of what follows, but we also have another goal: to teach you how *to be* human in an inhuman world. To help you become a *creator* of oases—a froggy friend to other weary and lonely frogs.

So, our purpose is twofold. To comfort and welcome the weary and the lonely, and to help them become comforters of others. We will show you how a human can live in an inhuman world, and how to be a true human to others.

A MAP FOR OUR JOURNEY

Let me draw a map to help orient you for this journey. Our destination is to become more truly human, even in a world that is hostile to humanity. To be "truly human" means to be like Jesus. That's our goal.

This begs two questions: first, "What is Jesus (aka God) like?" And second, "How do we become like that?" In our way of thinking, the first question answers the second. Coming to know and be with Jesus as he really is, is the way he changes us to be like him. Or in the odd frog language I'm using here, finding and resting with our biggest Froggy friend, Jesus, we become little froggy friends to others.

So, what *is* Jesus (aka God) like? We'll unpack this more later, but for now, let me draw your attention to Jesus' title, Immanuel, which means "God with us."

Jesus, the full revelation of God and the "exact expression of his nature,"[2] is the kind of guy who wants to be *with* us–*with you*! He wants to be with us in our joy and our pain. In our good and our bad. In our dressed-up Sunday best and in our worst sinful binges.

We have a word for this kind of intense desire to be with someone and help them no matter what: **compassion**. "Compassion" means to "suffer with" another person, but it's more than just feeling bad for someone! It's a deep inner drive—which flows from a loving heart—that propels us toward someone to share in their suffering, sorrow, and pain, but also in their joy and happiness.

Compassion simply cannot stand back and watch someone hurt (or be happy)! Compassion feels "compelled" to act. Even if all I can do is sit with someone and cry with them, compassion must act. Compassion always pushes me to engage in other people's lives. Compassion creates deep connection between people.

But compassion is not a blind bleeding-heart response to suffering. It's *a wise* bleeding-heart response. Wisdom wonders things like, "What is the truth in this situation? Why is this person hurting? How can I help most effectively? Might this suffering also have good results?" True

---
[2] Hebrews 1:3 CSB

compassion not only deeply desires to help, but also discerns the best way to help and then does it.

And that's Jesus. Jesus *is compassion*. Jesus is Immanuel–God with us. Compassion propelled God to become a frail human with us. His own compassion "compelled" him to suffer *with* us and to suffer *for* us so that he could rescue us from that suffering.

That's what Jesus (God) is like. He is a deep well of compassion for all of us. An oasis of wise and tender care in a vast uncaring desert. That's our goal. To become oases for others, connected to The Oasis himself through streams of living water in the desert.

To be human in an inhuman world means to be compassionate.

Easy, right? Now that you know how to be human in an inhuman world, you can just go do it, right? Why'd you waste your money on this book? Just go "be compassionate as your [Heavenly] Father is compassionate."[3]

Because you know it's not easy! We wrote this book for you because we know compassion is scary and hard! Authentic compassion requires me to hurt when I see someone hurt, to be joyful when I see someone joyful. I must enter into another person's life and share it with them. I don't have the energy for that! I'm hurting too badly myself. I've got my own struggles, my own needs. Compassion requires me to be vulnerable! But I've got to keep my defenses up or I'll be overwhelmed!

---

[3] Luke 6:36 CEB

I know, (froggy) friend, *I know*. I feel the same way! But I'm not asking you to give compassion to others without first having *received compassion*. You don't have to give away something you don't have, and you don't have to do it alone!

"But," my fear screams, "receiving compassion is no easier!" It means being needy, being seen as weak or even bad. What does it say about me that I need compassion– that I need help? I get this one too! We'll tackle all of this in the next few chapters, but here's the tl;dr (too long; didn't read) version.

The first step in overcoming all these difficulties is coming to experience God as *actually good*. God loves me (and you!). God *likes* me (and you)! He *delights* in me (and you!). I can trust that whatever he does is for my good, and no matter what atrocities I do, he will forgive me, help me, and nurse me back to health. I am God's beloved child. That's why Jesus died for me (and for you), because we are and always have been his dearly beloved! God is compelled by his compassion to help us!

The second step is admitting I need compassion, just like everyone else. I need help. I don't naturally trust God, and I feel I must go it alone. I have to admit that I'm frail and weak and cynical, and that in the name of self-protection or self-sufficiency or self-soothing, I'll do just about any sin.

I know this is difficult to admit. It's much easier to blame it all on the world or my parents or the government or Adam and Eve or whomever. To be sure, they bear some of the blame. But I'm also to blame. I can't begin to be healthy in this world without properly placing the blame—and that means honestly admitting my own burden of guilt as well as that of others.

Please note, it's much easier to admit my guilt boldly if I have first come to know God as *truly good*! When I know Jesus as God *with* me—God for me—then I know his response to my pain and sin will always be compassion. Going to him, cap in hand, saying "Lord, have mercy!" is the safest thing in all the world. It's the best thing in the world! He will always accept me, pick me up, wash me off, and heal me. *Somehow*, he will make all the bad stuff I did into beauty and good.

I know for many people the previous lines are all too familiar. They may be words you've said so often you don't really hear them as being about a real flesh-and-blood God anymore. For others, the love of Jesus has been weaponized against you by an abusive church or family. You've had to say the right things about Jesus while being hurt, forced, and manipulated.

But for just a moment I invite you to hope that Jesus is really different from all of that. To imagine that Jesus really is God driven by compassion. That he came on a rescue mission to save the apple of God's eye: you!

We'll come back to this, but for now I wonder if you can catch a glimpse of this beautiful truth: God is in love with you like a good dad is in love with his little daughter. He's come to hunt down all the evil that threatens you. When you run away, or when you kick and scream because you can't see how good he is, that's okay, he understands, and he's going to continue patiently and gently protecting, waiting for, and pursuing you. When you finally relent, he'll sweep you up in his arms, kiss your cheek, and fix you all up! And he'll do that over and over and over again!

That's a brief sketch of this book. I learn to be compassionate by first learning to receive compassion from God. From there I can have compassion on other people because I can see they need it just as badly as I do.

It's all a big positive feedback loop. First, I'm plunged deep into the gentle, compassionate love of Jesus (usually through an encounter with another person who has already been there), and that makes it safe for me to love others a bit like Jesus loves me which plunges them into the compassion of Jesus!

I must point out that this feedback loop is the loop we continually live in. It's not a one-time experience! I am continually being shown compassion, trusting God, and dropping myself into his arms. I'm like a frog swimming in circles around the deep pond of God's love, gathering froggy friends along the way. Or, enough of this frog stuff, I'm like a hawk riding the powerful updraft of Christ's love, gathering hawky friends on the way back to my heavenly home.

So "to be human in an inhuman world" means to be loved by Jesus and then, empowered by his Spirit, to love like Jesus. It means to let Jesus love me in my pain, in my sin, and in my loneliness and then to love others in their pain, their sin, and their loneliness.

That's why we wrote this book. That's why Liv and I started Signpost Inn Ministries. We want to create oases for weary life-travelers as others have done for us. Our "Inn" isn't necessarily a physical place. It's anywhere a few frogs (or hawks!) have gathered together to share Jesus' compassion with each other.

Are you tired and burdened? Are you lonely? Hurt? Lost? Are you standing at a crossroads in life wondering what the hell to do next and where on earth God is? Then we invite you to pause and look to the side of the road. There stands our little inn (or pond, or eyrie, take your pick). All the lights are on. The front door is wide open. You can hear singing and laughter, and you can smell fresh bread being pulled from the oven. Join us. Then start your own inn.

2

WHAT'S WRONG WITH THE WORLD?

Brandon

I have set myself a difficult task for this chapter. I want to convince you that the Christian teaching about "original sin" is exceedingly *good* news. That it creates extraordinary compassion for ourselves and others. That it is uniquely powerful at unifying people across impossible divides. That it is, in fact, *necessary* to believe in original sin to be human in this inhuman world.

But let's start more simply. What are humans? What am I? I am God's beloved creation, made for eternal, intimate companionship with God and others. I am made to be loved and to love, to know fully and be fully known, to be "at home" here and everywhere.

The first two chapters of the Bible lay this out. But I can also feel the truth of these statements deep in my bones. Everything in me desires to be "at home."

Beyond my desire for wealth lies the desire for total security. Underneath my desire for sex lies the desire to be accepted and cherished just as I am. Inside my desire for food is the desire to be sustained and provided for by the world. And beneath all these desires lies an even deeper longing. A longing that has never been satisfied: the desire to be intertwined with beauty itself, to somehow be both inside it and outside it at the same time. To *become* it and at the same time *behold* it.

Perhaps you've experienced this strange desire once or twice in your life. If you've ever seen the stars from the top of a mountain on a cloudless night and wanted to dive into them, you know what this desire feels like. Or if you've gazed on your newborn son and wanted to simultaneously see him become his own man *and* absorb him into your own being and never let him go. Or if you've looked at your wife and felt the paradoxical longing to meld into her as one, and yet remain yourself so that you can appreciate the experience! Then you know what this deep longing feels like.

Paradoxically, suffering reveals my longing for home even more than happiness. In suffering and sadness I know that something is missing. That the world is not supposed to be this way. That I'm not home but I *should* be.

C.S. Lewis explains this feeling: "We are on the outside of the world, the wrong side of the door. We discern the freshness and purity of morning, but they do not make us fresh and pure. We cannot mingle with the splendors we see."

"But," he says, "all the leaves of the New Testament are rustling with the rumor that it will not always be so. Some day, God willing, we shall get *in*."[1]

Our desire to be home, to get "in," is our desire for God. It is the afterglow of Eden. Somewhere deep inside every human is the ancestral memory of paradise. We were made for love. We were made for intimacy. We were made *for God*.

But something has gone horribly, horribly wrong. We long for peace, but there is no peace to be found. We long for love, but whatever love we find is fickle and unstable. We long for intimacy, but we are always alone inside our heads.

Still, this deep sense of loss—this deep longing for home—is only part of our experience. Right alongside my deep longing for *home* is another desire. A dark and evil desire for destruction, for death and chaos and pain. I find myself drawn to darkness. I take perverse pleasure in other people's pain. No matter how hard I want to resist, I find that I also don't want to resist.

If you read that last paragraph and did not resonate, then you are not being honest. Everyone is conflicted. No one is free from dark desires. As Aleksandr Solzhenitsyn lamented from within the Soviet gulag: "If only there were evil people somewhere insidiously committing evil deeds, and it were

---
[1] *The Weight of Glory*

necessary only to separate them from the rest of us and destroy them. But the line dividing good and evil cuts through the heart of *every* human being."

There are no simply "good" and simply "evil" people. There is no "us versus them." Evil is not merely "out there" in the structures and systems of the world; it is also "in here," inside of me and of you. Given the right circumstances you too would have been a willing Nazi, or a member of the Khmer Rouge, or a supremacist. Evil has corrupted the heart of every human. Specifically, it has corrupted our very organ of desire. We not only enjoy evil, we discover that we *want* to enjoy it.

All of this is included in the Christian teaching on original sin.

IT GETS WORSE BEFORE IT GETS BETTER

Let me unpack this a little bit more. I promise, the good news is coming, but we need to understand who we are before we can understand how this could ever be good news.

I'm a beloved child of God, created for love, for intimacy, for glory, *for God*, yes, but I am also the avowed enemy of all that is good and beautiful and true—all that is holy—all that is God. I am a tragedy. A beautiful work of art, though vandalized from without and within.

When Christians talk about "sin," it is this state of our hearts we primarily have in mind. We are trying to describe this fundamental discovery of our own experience: something inside us is so broken, so corrupted, that we cannot escape its effects. Sin is like a gravitational field through which everything we do, say, and think passes and gets bent. "Sin" is a controlling reality that leads us inevitably to selfish and destructive actions.

We are powerless over it. I know it's not supposed to be that way. I don't want it to be that way… except… I *do!* This is Sin. Its pull within us bends our every desire and choice.

This is the source of my guilt before God. I am guilty not only in my overt acts of disobedience, but because the state of my heart is to desire to do them and to delight in doing them. My guilt is in my *desire* to destroy what he loves and to pervert what he has made beautiful and innocent.

That is original sin. That's what truly separates me from God. That's what damns me. I discover that I am the kind of being that loves dark and perverse things.

It's not God who damns me. It's me. I don't *want* to be around God. It's not God who casts me into Hell; I cast God into Heaven and tell him to stay put, and so create my own Hell.

It's crazy, I know. It's irrational, I know. But it's a biblical truth that doesn't need any faith to believe. You can see the evidence in yourself. This world is inhospitable to humans because each of us makes it so. We are still beloved creations of God, though broken and corrupted. We are still good insofar as we are created by God to be like him, but evil insofar as we have lost our ability to act like it. We still have some sense that we need to love and be loved, but we find another law at work in our souls. We have some kind of "instinct" that constantly turns us inward on ourselves.

We really, *really*, can't escape ourselves. I am powerless

over my dark side. I was born with it, and in an important sense, I *am it*.

It's this powerlessness that the doctrine of original sin is describing. My organ of desire—my heart—is broken. My heart is twisted away from God and others and into myself.

HOW IS THIS GOOD NEWS?

If all I have to say is we're helplessly and hopelessly self-centered, that isn't good news. It's not even "news"; it's what we already know through daily experience. The good news is that God has responded and continues to respond compassionately to us in our poor, miserable state!

Our hearts are broken cisterns dug in a desert. Dark, dry, and cavernous. We cannot hold water or be an oasis for others. We can only consume. But God is a gushing spring in the desert. He is a mighty river overflowing its banks. It turns the parched dirt into fertile soil, and wherever it finds a hole—a cracked and empty cistern—it rushes in all the faster!

The deeper our depravity, the greater God's compassion. The wider our cracks, the faster God's love can flow *through* us to others. The good news is that we are helpless to help ourselves, and this breaks our Good Father's heart, so he comes *rushing* to help us.

Jesus is compassion incarnate. We are unable to love God and others ahead of ourselves. So Jesus did. We are incapable of saying "no" to our own craven desires and the devil. So Jesus did. We cannot change our hearts. So Jesus does it for us.

Our sinful selfishness does not repulse God; it *attracts* him! Much like a screaming, angry toddler who selfishly wants his sister's lollipop *somehow* attracts his mother's heart rather than repels it, so God has come rushing to our aid with love, even in the middle of our tantrum.

The good news is that compassion, a heart-felt compulsion to comfort and help, is the *correct* response to human sinfulness. It is God's motivation for becoming human in Jesus.

To live like a true human—like Jesus—in an inhuman world is to have compassion for others.

You are helplessly selfish (just like me), but you are still God's beloved child, and he cannot stand seeing you held back by your sin. You were meant to be glorious, loving, and kind (just like Jesus). So he rushes to help you—to free you from your bondage to sin. And we are all invited to join him in being compassionate.

Compassion is the motivation, and hospitality is what it motivates.

Jesus didn't just come rushing to our aid, to bandage our broken bones and disappear. No, he made his home among us. He dwells with us. His spirit lives in us *and we in him!*

Hospitality is incarnate grace. It is compassion given to another by opening a door, offering a meal, sharing a glass of wine. Hospitality, in all its concrete particulars that we will explore in detail later, is forgiveness and love embodied. We might say that Jesus *is* hospitality—he is compassion embodied. He has opened himself to us and allowed us to dwell in his heart. We are welcomed home in Jesus.

Every act of our own hospitality is an extension of this. We never welcome someone into *our* home; we are always welcoming a fellow traveler into *Jesus*.

Hospitality bridges every divide between us. We are all the same. We are all lost and weary travelers who desperately need a home. As soon as we recognize that, we can no longer hate "them" for not being like "us." They *are* us, and we *are* them! We can see their desperate need for hospitality and hear the call to rush to their aid. Then we can welcome them into our lives. We all need someone to welcome us home into Jesus' heart.

3

THE FIRST PLACE WE MEET GOD

Liv

The first place we meet God is in another person. God is loving, welcoming, full of gut-level compassion for us, but our poor sin-sick fallen hearts just can't believe that. It takes an outside force to reveal the truth that the Lord of Everything pursues me because he doesn't want to be without me. No agenda. Just love. Love like we've never known. Until him. But our blind eyes, hard hearts and tightly closed fists do not know how to open to his love. We can't even know that he's trustworthy.

So I have you over to dinner. It's super awkward to accept, because you don't know me very well. We've only seen each other a handful of times throughout the semester at our kids' karate classes. But somehow it seems possible.

You come over, offering fruit salad to add to the cookout. My sons are tearing around the house with Nerf swords; your son joins them. Off they go.

We chop up burger toppings and ask the social questions:

"And you grew up in Maryland?"

"Oh, yeah, two sisters…."

"No, never did get to keep the St. Bernard."

We find out what we have in common. The men are starting up the grill. We get our drinks and bring some out to the guys. The days are warming up. We're all ready to get back out on the river.

No requirement. No program. You know we're Christians, even the kind with a crucifix on our wall, but we don't start there. The welcome is enough. As little as this seems, you are meeting God in me. God who loves burgers and beer. God who loves laughing and St. Bernards. I met the Lord through my parents' joy and continue to meet him in Scripture and the sacraments, ever developing and changing in my understanding of who he is and how much bigger and bigger he gets the more you live in him. You may not know it yet, but that's who you're having a cookout with.

We're not born with the instinct to trust God. Even our trust of humans is limited. It takes practice; it takes modeling. We all first learn what forgiveness is through a human who accepts our apology and sincerely forgives us, leaving the sin behind and preserving the relationship. By extension, we begin to believe that when God says he forgives, it's the same experience—only more so! We develop muscle memory for kindness, generosity, mercy by experiencing these in believers – the Lord's people. Then when you start to read his words for yourself and come across "underneath are the everlasting arms,"[1] you remember the safe arms you have known, the strong ones ready to catch you when you jumped from the edge of the pool. The Holy Spirit breathes faith into us: new instincts that default to trust in this Lord of Creation and surrender to the Captain of the Heavenly Armies who, you now know, fights for you!

Think about that! My home is where Heaven meets Earth, where humans can really know that acceptance is real; forgiveness is real; Jesus is real. It's like communion! Home matters! It's what we all long for. Home, where people meet God through other people, is central to being human. It is, of course, also central to being a Hobbit.

If you're not sure that home is really that important, I offer Rosie Cotton. Here's what she says to Sam after he has returned from his adventure and finally gotten up the nerve to speak to her, "'Well, you've wasted a year, so why wait longer?' 'Wasted?' I says. 'I wouldn't call it that.' Still, I see what she means."

In this "wasted" year, while Rosie waited for him to return and make his move, Sam followed Frodo from the Shire, skipped meals!, killed a monster spider, briefly bore (uncorrupted) the Ring of Power, and finally spoke the words that make us all cry, "Come, Mr. Frodo! I can't carry

---

[1] Deuteronomy 33:27 "The God of old is your dwelling place, and underneath are the everlasting arms." ESV

it for you, but I can carry you!" And so saved Middle Earth. Then he came home. To do what really matters.

Certainly great acts of heroism and bravery, loyalty and persistence also teach us about the heart of our God, but all of these things are FOR something else. Jesus bore an unspeakable load, faithful to the excruciating end. Why? It was more than bravery. It was for love, for joy, for you. And what's the goal of the Fellowship of the Ring? What does Boromir's death buy? Why does Gandalf fight the Balrog? It was all for Rosie Cotton.

If you don't believe me, listen to Tolkien's own words concluding the saga:

> But Sam turned to Bywater, and so came back up the Hill, as day was ending once more. And he went on, and there was yellow light, and fire within; and the evening meal was ready, and he was expected. And Rose drew him in, and set him in his chair, and put little Elanor upon his lap.
>
> He drew a deep breath. 'Well, I'm back,' he said.[2]

"Home" is the hero's reward. It's where the struggle ends. Where we belong. It's a comfy chair, a warm fire, a giggling child. Home is what it's *all* for. It is all for Rosie Cotton.

---

[2] The very last page of *The Return of the King* by J.R.R. Tolkein

YOU SERVE ROSIE COTTON

Here's what I'm saying:

You may want to be Aragorn (I know I do!). To set off and destroy all the bad guys. But remember you are a servant of Rosie Cotton. Your bravery safeguards the home—where we first meet God in another person. You are preserving culture, belonging, the home, which is the source of all the good stuff. Honor and participate in what you fight to preserve.

If you already resonate with the desire to be the welcome or to receive it, you're absolutely right to! Never belittle or sell it short. You are doing the unbelievable work of participating in love and welcome—the very heart of who God is, the very stuff that life is made of! What sane person ever said, "The Shire is a waste of time" or "Stay-At-Hobbit-Hole-Moms are lame"??

PRACTICE

Think of a welcome you have received. Even meeting for coffee or going for a walk. What physical things do you remember of that encounter? How long ago was it? Have you ever told anyone else about it? Write briefly about the lasting effect that welcoming encounter had. Do you think the person knows how formative it was for you? Drop them a quick line of thanks.

4

WHAT GETS IN OUR WAY

Brandon

Why do we struggle to be stay-at-hobbit-hole-people? Why are we always striving so hard to be something that we aren't?

For me, it's because I believe I'm unlovable. I constantly tell myself that I'm incompetent, stupid, and alone. I believe if you really knew me, you wouldn't like me. After all, I know me, and I don't like me, so why would you?

So, I spend most of my days working hard to project an image of a smart, successful, likable person. Someone I think I could accept so you will too. It's terribly exhausting! I feel there's no place to rest. Nowhere I can drop my pretension. There's no "home" for the real me. Do you feel the same?

How did I get here?

I've discovered one of the reasons. It's because the story I'm telling myself about myself doesn't match reality. I can't see my home because I don't believe it could exist. Even when I'm sitting with my wife, the one person who knows me best—*and still loves me*—there is a running commentary in my head saying, "But you don't deserve it; she doesn't *really* know you. You're a f***ing loser!" (Yeah, my internal dialogue is pretty harsh!)

Do you also have a constant litany of negative thoughts about yourself playing in your head? I'm pretty sure you do.

I don't know anyone who doesn't. Most of the time we don't notice it, but it's there. A constant flow of thoughts and images that interpret our experiences. We're always telling ourselves a story about our lives while we're living them. It's how we make sense of life. And for most of us, the story we're telling ourselves about ourselves is pretty damn negative.

You can learn to notice the story you're telling yourself, though it might take a bit of practice. I encourage you to try it. First, take a "step back" from your thoughts. Notice that even as you are reading these sentences you have a steady stream of thoughts running through your head. Questions about what I'm saying, images and feelings that are associated with it, and assumptions about your own abilities, intelligence, safety, worth, etc.

Don't be surprised if your thoughts are a bit shy at first. It might help to close your eyes and take a few deep breaths; try not to judge, just notice. Sometimes it helps to change your context. Take a short walk or a shower. Sometimes I have to sneak up on my thoughts.

If you are really struggling with this, try not doing it all at once. Instead, set a reminder to go off a few times a day. Whenever it dings, take a moment to jot down what's going through your mind just then. What are you thinking? Feeling? Assuming? How are you interpreting the current situation? Pay special attention to your thoughts and judgements about yourself. After a few days you'll have a nice little sample of your background thought life.

What stories are you telling yourself about yourself? What "truths" do you repeat about yourself? What do you automatically assume others are thinking or saying about you? What do you automatically assume they *should* think about you?

As a spiritual director, I've heard a lot of people's self-narratives. I've noticed themes that repeat themselves. Here are some statements that other people often tell me they assume to be true about themselves. Do any of them hit home for you? Take a moment with this list. Circle the phrases that capture your own negative narratives.

- I am bad / evil
- I am disgusting
- I am unwanted
- I am unlovable
- I am not enough
- I am worthless

- I am unattractive
- I am not interesting
- I am incompetent
- I am inadequate
- I am weak
- I am not trustworthy
- I am cruel
- I am a burden
- I always mess up
- I am too much
- I don't matter
- I am depressing to be around
- _____ (write your own)

Take a moment with the items you circled on that list. Notice the feelings associated with what you wrote. Try not to judge them; just feel them.

Why do these feel so true to you? How have these beliefs helped you make sense of the world? Where did these narratives first start in your life?

If you feel comfortable doing so, try to recall some memories associated with these narratives and feelings. Don't push; simply let a memory rise to the surface. Pick a memory and describe what happened in one or two sentences.

Again, if you feel comfortable doing so, jot down the emotional and physical sensations you felt during that memory. For example, you might have felt anger, depression, hurt, sadness, frustration, fear, tension, nausea, shakiness, etc.

How did you try to make sense of that experience at the time? What conclusions did you draw about yourself? What story did you tell yourself about yourself?

Many of our negative narratives began as explanations for experiences we couldn't understand. Perhaps you decided you were a burden because your father was always busy and didn't seem to have time for you. Or maybe you figured that you were unattractive because your mother constantly commented on your size and need to exercise.

Or maybe you had an extremely embarrassing experience with a high-school girlfriend that made you feel stupid and you deeply internalized it by playing and replaying that experience over and over in your imagination for years (*not that that ever happened to me!*).

Or maybe, and please tread lightly here, you were a victim of abuse and made to feel shame for something that wasn't your fault.

Or maybe you are on the other side of this equation. You've hurt someone, betrayed someone, cheated on someone. Maybe your negative narrative has a basis in the reality of your sin.

Whew! You might be feeling overwhelmed right now. Please treat yourself gently here. I invite you to take a short break from reading. Go for a slow walk; look at something beautiful; listen to your favorite song; make yourself a tasty sandwich. There's no rush, I'll wait!

...

Welcome back. I hope you are doing okay! Identifying and facing our negative narratives can be hard work. Remember, you are not alone! Everyone has them!

Remember too, that even if they have some basis in reality, they aren't telling you the whole story. The truest truth about you is the one that Jesus tells. You are his beloved! You are forgiven! Worth giving his whole life to. He not only loves you, he *likes* you! We'll come back to this. But for now:

HOW MY NEGATIVE NARRATIVES AFFECT ME AND OTHERS

As we age, we embellish and re-tell negative narratives about ourselves. They become foundational to who we think we are and how we think the world works, and this negatively impacts the way we live our lives.

It's perfectly understandable! If what's unquestionably true about me is that I suck and am fatally flawed, then I will naturally try to compensate for, protect against, hide from, or paradoxically, verify my negative narrative. Let's take a quick look at each of these common responses:

1. Compensate: This is the most commonsense response. I work really hard to make up for my perceived fatal flaws. For example, as a child I might (wrongly) conclude, "Dad always comes home from work grumpy because my emotions are too much for him. I'm such a burden."

This then becomes a pattern for my life. I might work

constantly to meet other people's emotional needs while discounting and stuffing my own. I become a slave to my own inner critic that is always telling me, "You're too much!"

2. Protect: Another sensible response to inner criticism is to go on the offensive. When a voice inside of me keeps saying, "Everybody thinks you're weak and pathetic! They'll hurt you the first chance they get!" my response might understandably be, "Not if I can hurt them first!"

3. Hide: The opposite of playing offense is to play defense. Run! Isolate! Disappear! Never let them know how I really feel! "I always mess up" or "I'm disgusting," so I better stay away from the group and avoid any responsibility.

4. Verify: Paradoxically I might try to embrace my negative narrative. In a chaotic world of suffering, my self-critical belief is the only thing I know for certain. I may not understand why my family life is crazy, and I can never be sure of being right or wrong, but at least I *know* that I'm cruel/don't matter/weak.

I wrap this narrative around myself like a security blanket and lean into the identity it provides. It's an if-you-can't-beat-'em-join-'em move. We say something like, "Oh, so you think I'm bad!? Well fine! I'LL SHOW YOU BAD!" Or "I am so weak, I can't do much of anything for myself, so it's best not to ever try."

Here's what all these responses have in common. They are projections of fake personas. They are attempts to cover up what I think I really am with a mask that will somehow keep me safe or make me significant.

They are all attempts to disguise myself from myself so I can live with myself. I'm driven to pretend to be someone I'm not because I can't stand the person I think that I am.

Let me say again that this is all quite common! You are not alone! If you are nodding your head saying, "Yep, that's me. Nailed it," you probably also have another layer of negative self-talk going right now saying, "See, you *are* the worst! You have a real problem with negative self-talk, don't you!"

Pause. Breathe. It's okay. You are not alone! You're normal. We are all trying to escape our negative narratives somehow. I invite you to gently accept some compassionate understanding for all that's going on inside of you all the time.

Still with me? Good to keep going? Alright then, buckle up, because we must cover one more difficult topic.

HOW PRETENDING TO BE SOMEONE I'M NOT BECOMES MANIPULATIVE AND COERCIVE

Unfortunately, my play-acts are not only for myself; they are also attempts to control how others perceive and treat me. Why? Because I can't stop needing to be loved, even if I believe I'm fundamentally unlovable. I can't stop needing to be significant, even if I think I'm fundamentally worthless. I can't stop being human, and I have to get my needs met somehow! So I manipulate or coerce others.

This is perfectly understandable. Think about it. I'm afraid that I'm pathetically incompetent. I'm terrified that if you knew "the truth" about me, you'd toss me away like the trash that I "really" am. So I have learned to compensate. I strive to be someone who appears extremely competent and therefore desirable.

I *need* you to see me as brilliant, as knowing everything, so I'm sorely tempted to embarrass and ridicule someone else to appear more competent. It can be really disgusting.

All this becomes a self-reenforcing feedback cycle. I need you to think of me as lovable, so I manipulate you, which is evidence that I'm unlovable, so I work harder to make you think of me as lovable… and now I'm trapped in a loop.

Worse still, even though so much of our hurtful behavior is understandable, it's still inexcusable. I'm never justified in manipulating or coercing another person, even if I'm afraid. What starts as a coping mechanism quickly becomes a weapon of mass destruction, and we are all guilty of hurting others.

WHAT NOW?

This chapter has been mostly diagnosis. My negative narratives are a big reason that I behave in selfish and unloving ways. It's hard to find an oasis full of froggy friends if I can never trust anyone, and it's impossible to build an oasis for other froggy friends if I'm only doing it to get my own needs met!

Knowing this does nothing to help me overcome it! How do I let go of my negative narratives and learn to be loved and to love? The short answer is "Jesus!" We'll unpack that answer in a later chapter. For now, I encourage you to talk to Jesus about what you've learned from this chapter. What core beliefs do you hold onto about yourself? What core need do you feel must get met? How has that driven you to manipulate or coerce others?

Jesus forgives and loves you! It may be hard to feel that's true right now, but that's okay. Hold on. Trust him. He will never forsake you.

PRACTICE

Henri Nouwen had a helpful and unique take on this idea. He summarized our negative narratives into three lies we all tend to believe about ourselves.

Lie 1: I am what I do. Security and significance come by accomplishing things. I have to finish all the tasks on my list or get good grades or that promotion. I have to be strong or thin. My kids have to be successful. Etc.

Lie 2: I am what I have. Security and significance come by having stuff. I'm good if I have lots of money or responsibilities or fancy titles. I'm safe if I have a good retirement plan and a big house. Etc.

Lie 3: I am what others say or think about me. Security and significance come by having people think well of me. I need a good reputation or to have everyone like me. I need to be considered the expert or the best at what I do.[1]

---

[1] "Being the Beloved" Sermon Given in 1992
https://www.youtube.com/watch?v=trG7Oh_PopM

Take a few minutes with these lies. Which one most resonates with you? Which one do you most often find yourself believing? We all believe them all at some point, but one of them tends to be our "home."

How do you see this lie play out in your life? In what ways do you attempt to prove your significance or establish your security based on the primary lie you believe?

For example, if my negative narrative says, "I'm not enough," I am likely to believe the lie that "I am what others say or think about me." I might try to be excessively helpful, always trying to help others but never letting anyone help me. I force others to need me as a way of protecting myself against being thought of as inadequate.

Finally, take a moment to consider what unhealthy or sinful habitual or compulsive behaviors you often engage in. How might these be related to trying to protect, hide, compensate for, or verify your negative narratives?

Who do you pretend to be to force others to meet your core needs?

5

LIES WE HOLD ONTO

Liv

I had a teddy bear named Edward. My aunt gave him to me in 1981. By 1990, he was totally flat since I slept with him or on him every single night. Then, in 2018, I stayed at a hotel in Minnesota for a conference, and I lost him. Do the math; that's a lot of years of companionship suddenly gone.

When, after calls and frantic searching in case I'd left him somewhere in the house, I finally had to accept that he was truly gone. I sat on the end of my bed; Brandon sat down at my side, and I cried and I cried and I cried. Brandon knew better than to say, "It was just a stuffed animal," or "You're disturbingly old to care so much about a toy." He just let me cry until I was all done.

Then I started putting words together about how I really

felt. He wasn't my pillow or my favorite toy; he was the only thing that, for as long as I could remember, had unconditionally loved me.

As the words left my mouth, I realized there was a reason he was gone. Although I knew of course that Edward didn't actually love me, I believed that if anyone did, it was my bear. Because no one else did. I was unlovable.

There are lies we hold onto, even comfort ourselves with—narratives we're unwilling to let go of because, backward as it seems, our negative inner story answers a question about what we fear most. I fear I'm unlovable; I hang onto Edward who means unconditional love. And when things are hard for a minute in real life? There's my answer. I'm unlovable. Only Edward loves me. Everybody hates me. Guess I'll go eat worms.

The lies we hold onto might be part-truths, but fear inflates them into fundamental truths, truths that make me who I am. I *was* a lot as a kid. Loud, big, social, emotional, hard to love. I (understandably) exasperated my parents. I thought that I was too much for them. My instinct was to withdraw, to invest in my friendships, to ride my bike a lot. And when I slept, Edward—always there—held the impression of acceptance that was unmoved by my turbulence. That longing for understanding could settle down inside me as I held onto Edward. Everything around me seemed uncertain. At least I knew I was unlovable.

I grew up eventually, so when I blurted out my childish belief about Edward loving me unconditionally, I saw clearly that I was very wrong about him. Very wrong about my need for acceptance being met by this furry little guy while no one else wanted me around. His comfort wasn't actually confirmation that I was unlovable. He was just fuzz and stuffing which made him comfy to hold onto.

(In case I'm making you too sad, you should know I've created an ending to Edward's story where he escapes from the hotel dumpster and runs off happily, a real cinnamon-colored bear in the far Northern woods among his Minnesota brothers, à la Velveteen Rabbit. Not better?)

You see, we hang onto self-judgment because it feels like who we are. We've held these seeming-truths for so long, we can't imagine Self without them. "I may not know much, but I know I'm a fake." "I have a bad feeling; it must be because I'm a coward." "Of course she looked at me weird; I'm too self-absorbed."

Hanging onto these lies, though, means we never get to address what we believe about ourselves and maybe challenge it. Our lies are so important to our sense of self that we feel we can't go there. We can't open them up, take them apart, see if there's anything real in there. I held onto Edward and my fear that love was conditional, that if anyone knew the real me, I could make them not love me. That bit of myself—fearful, lonely, bad—was never released, seen, given space, maybe even healed. So, I believed things about myself that may not have been true in exactly the way I feared. Love was not unavailable.

If you haven't read Donna Tartt's *The Goldfinch*, you don't really have to, unless you can stomach a very dark tale. I read it for the second time recently because it had grabbed me the first, though I couldn't put my finger on why. This time I think I get it. Spoiler alert: I am going to reveal the secret of the book, so if you plan to read it, skip to the asterisk*. Briefly: Theo as a young boy accidentally steals a priceless painting during a disaster in which his mother dies. He cannot find a way to return it but instead wraps it in paper and puts it permanently in storage, paying in cash every two years to keep it safe. Because of this secret, Theo believes himself fundamentally untrustworthy, sneaky, isolated, permanently inferior.

The painting is Theo's negative inner narrative. He isn't storing the painting itself; he's storing his shame at being so flawed. He describes his wrapping job as "insane": layers of paper, a bag, packing tape round and round and round until its corners are soft, and it could be anything. Theo's cocoon holds all his self-doubt, all his fear, all his panic at being left suddenly alone in the world—and it's all his fault. It must stay in cool storage, untouched, untouchable, eternal, immutable, permanent. A truth unchanging. A lie that defines him.

Theo lives as a puppet, controlled by the bundle in the locker—his belief that he has caused his isolation. But here's the thing: Theo hasn't had the painting for decades. It was stolen out of its insane cocoon when he was a teenager. Finding this out near the end of the story, Theo races to the storage unit and unwraps—well, I'll leave a little bit untold. The important element is that when he dares to undo this burden, when he busts it open, it does not hold what he thought it did. He is not who he thought he was.

The defining secret of his life is simply not so. He doesn't know who he is. What might his life have been like if Theo had not believed these lies of himself? Theo's mother had adored him. He was the center of her attention and affection. What if he had been able to continue living in that love and acceptance? Believing what was real: he was loved no matter what kind of trouble he got himself into.

*I see these burdens, Theo's and mine, as a kind of abscess, an infection that the body keeps unresolved by building a barrier around it. We think we've kept something essential to our survival, but all we've created is a walled-off mass of unfulfilled needs that must remain inviolate and so unhealed. Don't poke holes in the narrative. And if you do? Well, I don't know if you've ever seen a lanced abscess ...

These self-defining lies don't help you; they offer no comfort; they give no wisdom, no real certainty, no control. Bleak, perhaps, but true. And not without hope!

The lies I hold onto don't define me, and I don't have to carry them forever. I can be me without hanging on to my negative narrative. Healed, I can be the real me! There is freedom and soul-health when we let the Lord lance these abscesses, draining their power. Nothing of our real selves is lost when we stop believing our own lies.

When Edward loped off into the Northern Woods to be a Real Bear, I knew there was a reason he was gone. The Lord was being kind. I had to let go of the lies that I felt had defined me. Since 1981.

"I was a lot as a kid. Loud, big, social, emotional, hard to love. I (understandably) exasperated my parents. I saw that I was too much for them." This is not an entirely true narrative. It was not entirely true of myself. I may have been some of these things, but I was not, as I feared, fundamentally unlovable. What might have been if I'd come to believe myself lovable? Never too late to start.

There is a place where the real truth about ourselves is kept, immutable, eternal, permanent—the embrace of the Holy Spirit telling us through Isaiah, "I have loved you with an everlasting love." I am the little child that Jesus didn't turn away. He told everyone, "Hey! Don't leave her out. She's wonderful; Heaven was made for her." And the one who tells this truth has so much more to tell me about who he is, and who I am.

6

WHO IS GOD, REALLY?

Brandon

The key to knowing ourselves truly is truly knowing God. He tells us the truth about ourselves. He has given us an inheritance that is imperishable, undefiled, and unfading. He keeps my identity as one beloved and cared for by God safe in Heaven, immutably, eternally, permanently.[1] But that begs the question: Who is God, really?

To answer that question, we'll need to take a little journey back in time. Back to when Jesus was travelling around Israel with his disciples. Below, I'll recount one particularly important event from that time, and I invite you to come with me in your imagination. Read the story a few times,

---

[1] See 1 Peter 1:3-4

and as you do, immerse yourself in it. See the events in your mind's eye in full 3D. Smell the air; listen to the sounds and voices; feel the ground beneath your feet. Pay special attention to Jesus. Watch how he moves; hear the tone of his voice; notice the expressions on his face. Who is this person? What is he like? What does he care about?

Come with me:

> Not long after calling his disciples, Jesus went to the village of Nain. His disciples were with him, along with a large crowd of curious followers.
>
> As they approached the village gate, they met a large funeral procession—a young man's body was being carried on a simple wooden bier to be buried. He had obviously been a poor man, but well loved, as he had many grieving friends.
>
> Jesus stopped as the funeral procession came by. The dead man's mother followed close behind the body, weeping uncontrollably. She was a widow, and this was her only son. She had no one left in all the world.

Can you see it? Feel it? Now, pay attention, because this next bit is really important:

> When The Lord saw the widow weeping, his heart broke.

> Compelled by great compassion he approached her and said, "Please, don't cry." Then he grabbed hold of the bier. The pallbearers stopped. Whispers spread through the crowd. (Jesus had just defiled himself by touching the dead.)
>
> "Young man," Jesus said, "I tell you: wake up!"
>
> Immediately, the dead man sat up and began talking! Jesus helped him stand and joyfully gave him to his mother.
>
> Awe came over everyone, and they broke out in song and praises saying "Truly, God has come to help us!" And "This is a great prophet!"[2]

It's quite the story, isn't it? With such a wonderful ending! But I'd like to bring to your attention to who Luke says that Jesus is.

This is the first time Luke explicitly calls Jesus "The Lord." This is significant. Luke is calling Jesus, "Yahweh"—the God of the Old Testament—the God of Abraham, Isaac, and Jacob.

Luke is telling us who Jesus *is*. He's explicitly connecting Jesus to the God of the Old Testament who is the "Father of the fatherless and protector of widows." The one who "provides homes for those who are deserted" and leads prisoners out into prosperity.[3]

---

[2] Adapted from Luke 7:11-17
[3] Psalm 68:5-6 ESV

Jesus *is* God, and Jesus is the kind of person whose heart breaks at the funeral of a widow's only son. Jesus is the kind of person who can't just stand back and watch a mother weep. Jesus is the kind of person who has to *do something!*

That means God is that kind of person. God is driven by compassion. The Transcendent Creator's heart breaks at the sight of suffering. The Omniscient Ancient of Days notices when we are hurt, and he grieves. And The Almighty Maker of Heaven and Earth can't sit on the sidelines and watch. He has to *do something!*

The New Testament word translated as "compassion," means "moved to the bowels." Or, "moved so deeply you can feel it in your bones." You probably know what this feels like. You've seen someone in great suffering and felt your insides wrench.

Perhaps you've heard the crunch of a toddler's fingers slammed in a door and rushed to help. Or held a shaking friend whose father just died in a car crash. Or watched helplessly as a mother wept over her stillborn child.

That feeling. That feeling that you're going to throw up because someone else is hurting so badly. That feeling makes you say, "*I have to help!*" Sometimes it moves you before you can even think. You are on your feet running before you even have a plan. That's compassion. That's what Jesus felt. That's what *God* feels, even now, about *you*.

So, who is God, really?

I'll tell you who he's not. He's not a stodgy old man who lives "upstairs." He's not a bean counter keeping close account of your smallest infractions. He's not a system of propositions that you need to keep correctly organized.

He's a real, flesh-and-blood person.

He's a person who has suffered exhaustion, loss, and temptation. He's been abused, ridiculed, beaten, and even murdered. He's been abandoned. He's been required to sacrifice more than his human body and soul could handle. He gets it. He feels your pain.

God is the kind of person who, when he sees a mother crying over her dead son, immediately rushes to help. He's the first one to move. The first one to act. He's also the kind of person who can raise her son (and you) from the dead.

CAN THIS BE TRUE?

If you want to know what someone really believes, don't ask them. *Watch them.* I can say I love you, but if I don't act like it, then it's not true. If you want to know how God thinks and feels about you, watch what he does.

Here's another story adapted from Mark. Imagine yourself as one of the disciples watching this happen. Watch Jesus closely. How does Jesus move, what does he say, what emotions do you see on his face? Most importantly, what does he *do*?

> A man with leprosy came to him and, falling on his knees with his face in the dirt, he begged Jesus, saying, "If you are willing, you can make me clean." Moved with deep compassion, Jesus reached out his

> hand and touched the man's face. Lifting the man's eyes to meet his own, Jesus said, "I am willing, be made clean." Immediately the leprosy left him, and he was made clean.

What do you notice? How does Jesus—God—feel about this poor man? Why touch him? Perhaps because he hadn't been touched in years. Because Jesus empathized with his heart pain even more deeply than his physical pain, so he acted according to his word:

> The LORD helps all who fall;
> he raises up all who are oppressed.
> All eyes look to you,
> and you give them their food at the proper time.
> You open your hand
> and satisfy the desire of every living thing[4]

Jesus—God—*is willing* to come to your rescue. He is not disgusted by your disease or sin or addiction. On the contrary, the worse off you are, the more he wants to heal you.

You may believe that you are unlovable, but Jesus disagrees. He fondly loves you. His love does not *respond* to anything in you or that you do. God is too good for that. Instead, Jesus loved you before you even existed and hasn't ever stopped.

---

[4] Psalms 145:14-16 CSB

Can this be true, *really*? If you want to know, watch him! Of course, there is one place above all we should look to see what drives Jesus:

THE CROSS

Why did Jesus willingly suffer and die? What motivated him? Sadly, many of us can answer these questions without any emotion. As if they are quiz questions in Bible class or passwords into the "correct kind of Christianity." But Jesus' death and resurrection mean everything to him. We call it the "passion of Christ" for a reason.

Is there anyone in your life for whom you would be willing to die? Maybe your best friend? Hopefully your spouse? Certainly your kids if you have them. Try to imagine a situation where you deliberately choose to be tortured and die in the place of someone you love. Don't worry about whether you would actually have the courage to do it or not; imagine that you do.

What does it feel like to love someone that much? Where in your body do you feel that love?

I feel it in my chest. My heart swells, and my breathing deepens. Warmth spreads across my body from my heart to my legs and arms. For me, the moment of decision feels powerful. "Yes, yes I will take her place!"

I know what pain awaits me—and I'm afraid. I feel fear in my stomach. I feel sick. Like I'm going to puke. But the expanding warmth gives me strength. The discovery that I love her that much gives me determination. Bring. It. On.

As you are being led away to be tortured, what goes

through your mind? What are you thinking about this person for whom you're about to make the ultimate sacrifice? Again, don't get sidetracked by doubting your resolve. Just imagine you are brave enough to go through with it.

I think about all the things we've done together. The things I love about her; the things I hate about her. The great times, and the times that sucked. I don't have rose-colored glasses—she can be a real handful, but you know what? That makes this even better. I'm not dying for an angel. I'm dying for a real, complicated person. And my sacrifice is worth something because she needs me to do it for her.

Is this making sense? Jesus' death isn't a dry theological axiom. The passion story reveals God's deepest motivations. Jesus is a real human who journeyed through Hell and back for you. We've got to ask ourselves, why? What would motivate him to do that for us, for you? How does he feel about you? What does he think about you?

The correct answer is he "loves" you. But unless you're willing to engage your imagination, that will never hit home. "Love" can be such an empty word. For a moment, fill it with passion, with heart, with real blood and guts. Jesus loves you so much that he suffered Hell for you. *That's* how God feels about you. If you want to know how God feels about you, don't ask him, watch him.

Please pause with this. Take whatever time you need. Don't let this be an academic exercise. Meditate on the crucifixion and let your heart feel God's love for you.

WHAT ABOUT GOD'S WRATH?

"But," I can hear someone saying, "What about God's wrath?" Fair question. God sometimes says things like this in Ezekiel:

> I will pour out my indignation on you; I will blow the fire of my fury on you. I will hand you over to brutal men, skilled at destruction. You will be fuel for the fire. Your blood will be spilled within the land.[5]

How does that jive with Jesus' compassion? Quite nicely, actually. Only a few verses later in Ezekiel God makes it clear at whom these words are directed:

> Look, every prince of Israel within you has used his strength to shed blood. Father and mother are treated with contempt, and the resident alien is exploited within you. The fatherless and widow are oppressed in you. You despise my holy things and profane my Sabbaths…. One man within you commits a detestable act with his neighbor's wife; another defiles his daughter-in-law with depravity; and yet another violates his sister, his father's daughter. People who live in you accept bribes in order to shed blood.

---

[5] 21:31-32 ESV

> You take interest and profit on a loan and brutally extort your neighbors. You have forgotten me…[6]

God's wrath is terrible news! Unless you are a widow, or a slave, or an orphan. It's terrible news to those who extort, abuse, and rape. God's wrath is directed at all those who violate his beloved children, and that's fantastic news for their victims.

God's wrath and judgment are answers to the hardest question we face in life. Why so much injustice!? Why do the wicked prosper and the righteous suffer? Is there no justice?

Yes, there will be justice! God is good! He loves his created children so much that he cannot stand to watch them suffer! He *will* bring the hammer down on those that hurt and take advantage of his beloved creation.

But there's more! Even those doing evil are his beloved creation! He doesn't want them to die either! If only they would admit their sin he would touch them and heal them too! He says:

> Now as for you, son of man, say to the house of Israel, "You have said this: 'Our transgressions and our sins are heavy on us, and we are wasting away because of them! How then can we survive?'" Tell them, "As I live—this is the declaration of the Lord

---
[6] Ezekiel 22:6-12 ESV

> GOD—I take no pleasure in the death of the wicked, but rather that the wicked person should turn from his way and live. Repent, repent of your evil ways! Why will you die, house of Israel?"[7]

God is both compassionate *and* just. He is full of tender love for the oppressed *and* for the oppressors. God wants everyone to be healed, to repent and be restored to the joy of salvation. He earnestly invites all to come to him. He offers forgiveness and reconciliation freely and profusely. He also sternly warns us about the consequences of our actions so that we might be terrified and run back to his welcoming arms.

But if we will not listen to his urgent calls to repentance, then we invite his well-deserved punishment. We bring down his wrath upon ourselves.

God's wrath is not unjust or unfair. Nor is it capricious. It is driven by the very same goodness that drives his compassion. He is a good father who, watching his children abuse each other, wants them to reconcile, and wisely bears with them as long as necessary. But eventually, with those who insist on their wickedness, he will punish them.

Which am I? Am I the oppressed or the oppressor? Am I a child of God or his enemy? Which are you?

I'm both. We are all both. Because I am created by him, I am his beloved son. Because of the fall, I am his mortal

---

[7] Ezekiel 33:10-11 ESV

enemy. More on this later. For now, let's focus on the character of God.

What motivates God? Love. God *is* love.[8] And it is precisely the horrible predicament of sin that kindled God's compassion. Something had to be done! So Jesus did it. And he did it for everyone!

It's tragic when someone refuses to repent and accept God's love and compassion for them, and no one feels that tragedy more deeply than Jesus. As he said:

> Jerusalem, Jerusalem, who kills the prophets and stones those who are sent to her. How often I wanted to gather your children together, as a hen gathers her chicks under her wings, but you were not willing![9]

So who is God, really? God is good. God is just. God is *love*. God is Jesus.

PRACTICE: JOURNALING PROMPTS

How does meditating on the personality of Jesus change your perception of God's character? Write a prayer to God telling him how you feel about this chapter.

Read Exodus 34:3-7 below. I've replaced the name of God here with "Jesus." How do you feel when you read this? Write your thoughts and feelings as a prayer to Jesus.

---

[8] See John 15:13; 1 John 4 ESV
[9] Matthew 23:37 ESV

> The LORD came down in a cloud, stood with him there, and proclaimed his name, "Jesus." Then Jesus passed in front of him and proclaimed:
>
> The LORD – Jesus – is a compassionate and gracious God, slow to anger and abounding in faithful love and truth, maintaining faithful love to a thousand generations, forgiving iniquity, rebellion, and sin. But he will not leave the guilty unpunished, bringing the consequences of the fathers' iniquity on the children and grandchildren to the third and fourth generation.

Read Psalm 23 replacing any reference to God with "Jesus." As you read the Psalm consider what it says about how God—Jesus—feels about you. How does it make you feel to have God feel that way about you? (I also suggest you do this with Psalms 91, 86, 131, and with Isaiah 43).

Read Deuteronomy 10:12-22, again replacing references to God such as "the LORD" and "God" with "Jesus." How does that change your understanding of what God "requires of us"?

7

PRETENDING GOD IS SOMEONE HE'S NOT

Brandon

I love the smell of diesel. It's the smell of safety. It's the smell of Dad.

My dad was a railroad engineer. Like the trainmen of the old west, he ran trains from La Junta, Colorado to Dodge City, Kansas and to many other dusty outposts. He would be gone for a day or two at a time and come home smelling of steel and diesel. On the nights he came home late, I would often be half-asleep. The smell of diesel wafting into my room meant Dad was home, and all was well. To this day, the smell of diesel calms me. It smells like home.

Home means I'm safe. Home means I'm loved. Home is where Papa (what my kids call me) will always be there for me. No matter what happens—or what I do—Papa will always be on my side, working to make sure I have what I need. Sure, Papa can be big and scary, but not to me. To me he's strong and safe.

I know I'm lucky to have a good dad. So many people have terrible memories of their fathers. If you are one of these people, I'm sorry. Whether you never knew your father, or had a terrible one, being fatherless is tragic. Having a father committed to me means I'm never truly alone in this world, and nothing can fill the vacuum of being without one.

You can probably see where I'm going with this. God is supposed to be our good Father, but many of us feel abandoned, unsupported, or lost. Maybe God feels distant and aloof. Or maybe he feels uncaring and disinterested. Or maybe he feels rigid and demanding. These negative feelings about God are some of the biggest reasons we feel we're not home yet.

It's worth pointing out that we can replace the word "father" with "mother" here. Being motherless is just as "unhoming" as being fatherless. Many people have very real struggles with relating to God as masculine. In fact, this struggle is exactly my point.

Many of us struggle with trusting that God is good. We want to believe he loves us—that he *likes* us, but we often feel that God is cruel, manipulative, abusive.

Now, here's the kicker. Most of us feel strongly that we "should" love God. We "should" believe that he is good and caring. But is that how you really think God thinks about you? Is that how you really *feel* God *feels* about you? What is your "lived experience" with God?

I encourage you to take a moment of compassion for yourself with this question. Just as we have negative narratives about ourselves, we often have negative narratives about God. And just as we don't often notice our narratives about ourselves, we don't often notice the narratives we are telling ourselves about God.

We don't notice them for good reason. We often feel a lot of shame when we admit some of our negative feelings toward God. I have a strong intuition that *I shouldn't think or feel "that" about God! I'm supposed to believe that he's perfect, and kind, and loving!* But for a moment, please set those feelings aside. I have a lot of complicated feelings about God! Some positive, some negative.

What negative narratives about God play in the background of your mind? What negative experiences have shaped and drive those narratives? Be gentle with yourself as you explore this.

Let's take a little more time with this. Here is an exercise I have found very helpful.

DRAWING OUR THOUGHTS AND FEELINGS ABOUT GOD

For this exercise you are going to need a sheet of blank paper and some drawing supplies. A pen or pencil will work, but it's best if you also have some colored pencils or crayons or colored markers. Feel free to get as creative as you want!

Step 1: Take the blank sheet of paper and fold it in half so you have two equal sides. You're going to draw two "images" of God. On one side of the folded paper, draw your primary image of God. Use your dominant hand for this drawing (if you are right-handed that's your right hand; if you are left-handed that's your left hand). Your primary image of God is the one you feel most comfortable with—this is the image you would draw if I asked you in Sunday school, "what is God like" or "How *should* you think about God?"

This picture doesn't have to be realistic. You can draw symbols, or use colors, or even use words if you want. There isn't a wrong way to do this. Take a few minutes to draw.

Step 2: Now, spend a little time with the image that you just drew. What do you notice about it? What is surprising or new to you? How do you feel in your body when you notice those things? Jot down those thoughts and feelings somewhere on the page or in a journal.

Step 3: Next you're going to draw how you feel about God when it's safe to feel everything. God isn't going to get mad at you, and no one ever has to see this drawing. This is a chance to really let all your feelings about God surface, positive and negative.

Fold your paper over so your first drawing isn't visible. Now using your non-dominant hand and draw how you *feel* God is. Draw freely and intuitively, without worrying about the end result. Let your feelings rise to the surface and move you to express them on paper. Freely use color and abstract imagery; the point is to get in touch with those feelings and thoughts about God of which you might be afraid.

Step 4: Just as you did with the first image, spend a little time with this second image. What do you notice about it? What is surprising or new to you? How do you feel in your body when you notice those things? Jot down those thoughts and feelings somewhere on the page or in a journal.

Step 5: Now spread your page out and look at both images side by side. Compare and contrast the two images. What do you notice, wonder, or appreciate? How does your body feel as you notice these things? Jot your thoughts and feelings down on the page or in a journal.

...

If you just had a moment of panic about some of your feelings towards God, that's okay! I've done this exercise many times, and I still discover that I'm frequently angry, or cynical, or even disgusted with God. Some part of me often feels that he is distant, capricious, and even selfish.

If you have similar feelings, you're not alone! You're not a bad person or a bad Christian if you feel negative things about God. You are normal! We all have negative images of God. These false images of God come from our experiences with other people, suffering, and the things we've learned or been taught.

For example, experiencing great loss may lead us to believe that God is distant and doesn't care. Maybe we were taught that we are merely tools to be used by God, so we conclude that he only cares about us as long as we're useful and perform. Or we may have felt close to God at some point, but lost that feeling somewhere along the way, and now feel that God is holding out on us.

These negative feelings we have about God are also deeply connected to the negative narratives we believe about ourselves. They are two sides of the same coin. We project our judgments of ourselves onto God. How I think and feel about myself directly influences how I think and feel about God, and vice versa.

When I accept my own negative beliefs about myself as facts, they become indistinguishable from God's judgments of me. My expectations and demands on myself become God's expectations and demands.

I project onto God my own self-hate and my own impossible demands for perfection. I wind up with a crazy image of God. Perhaps I "should" believe that he is gracious, loving, and good, but I can't help feeling that he is stingy, cruel, and distant.

HOW OUR IMAGES OF GOD AFFECT OUR RELATIONSHIP WITH GOD

How we believe God feels about us dramatically affects how we feel about him. That affects my relationship with him. I have no desire to give thirty minutes a day to a God who thinks I'm disgusting. Or to a God who demands that I "give him time" like a needy, narcissistic boyfriend. Nor do I want to worship a God who tolerates me, but perpetually reminds me that I'm insufficient, like a crotchety grandmother who "loves" me, but always tells me how fat I am.

That makes sense! In my long ministry career, I have heard *many* people—young and old—complain that they struggle to love and obey God. When I make it safe for them to surface their true feelings about God—and their true beliefs about how God feels about them—I discover that the "god" they struggle to love and obey is a harsh, demanding, finger-wagging, narcissist who doesn't like them or care about them.

I usually respond, "Wow! I am so glad that you don't want to love and obey *that god*! Good job!"

That god doesn't exist. Except inside our own heads. He is a fictional character. We put our own negative narratives into his mouth, so they can be unalterable FACTS. If our own judgements of ourselves are God's honest truth, well then, I can't question them. "*God says* I'm a worthless good-for-nothing! *God says* I'm too much for anyone to put up with! *God says* I'm_____."

This begs the question: "What does God *actually* say about me?" We'll come to that question very soon. For now, I invite you to entertain the possibility that God doesn't say those things about you. What if God actually desires you? What if he is delighted by you? What if he feels deep, tender, compassion for you? What if he's not disappointed in you? What if God is proud of you?

How would that change your feelings toward him?

What if you and I aren't alone in this world? What if we're not orphans? What if God isn't gone? What if we have a papa, a *good father*, with us all the time? What if the whole world, even on the darkest and coldest nights, smells like diesel?

8

LEARNING TO SEE GOD CORRECTLY

Liv

The person behind the words matters so much. Think of that dreaded text: "Hey. Can we talk?" When it's from your passive aggressive boss while you're taking a sick day, you can be about sure you're losing your job. When it's your childhood friend who checks in once in a while out of curiosity and just to love you, merely glancing at their name popping up on your phone is a relief.

It's the same encountering God in his texts. If God is distant, if he thinks you're yucky, if he gets tired of your neediness, you might read him saying that he doesn't want you, even when he means the opposite. We can only hear him in the Word if we know him. And we can only grow in knowing him by reading the Word.

Just as we often meet God first in other people, we hear him first in the Bible. That's why Bible translations matter so much. It's good for a translation to be grammatically accurate, with an eye on historical context, the nuance of imagery, idiom and simile. But nothing matters in a translation more than presenting the Lord the way he wants to present himself to us. The translator must help us hear him, to know him through his words and actions.

Let's look at two examples—one New Testament and one Old Testament. I'm inviting you into an imaginative space here, where understanding who he is changes everything.

I have not yet encountered a more grievous instance of slander than the Latin Vulgate's rendering of Jesus' words to Mary Magdalene in the garden after the Resurrection. In the Latin, Jesus holds Mary off with the phrase "*Noli me tangere*" which in English is "Don't touch me." You'll see art that reflects this reading of his words, with Jesus sweeping off to one side and poor Mary kneeling or reaching for him and being told to keep her distance.

What cold, aloof ghost is this?! Mary, his friend, is weeping outside the gaping tomb, believing his dear body has been stolen, possibly desecrated. All her hope has been torn away. She'd give anything to hear his voice again. Through her tears she sees a figure and thinks it must be the groundskeeper. Sobbing, aching, broken, pathetic, she asks this worker if he knows where the body is. "Someone took my Lord away!" Nothing else matters, not even weeping and begging a stranger for help.

And then you have to hear the affection in his voice, the lump in his throat both with sorrow for her tears and joy for the imminent surprise when he speaks:

He says, eyes jovial, simply "Mary!" like he's waking her up from a nap. "Mary!" like she's heard a thousand times. "Mary!" like she's already had echoing in her brain since Friday afternoon when she had had to face the reality that she would never hear him say it again. The grieving mind is merciless. The very phrases and voices we cannot bear to hear because we long for them so deeply are the voices and phrases that jerk us out of daydreaming because we're sure we've just heard it again. Audibly? Or with the ears of the soul?

"Mary!" And she blinks back her tears. And sees the impossible. "Master!" And she falls toward him. She has to know with her hands that she hasn't actually dropped into madness with sorrow.

You know the Lord. Or you've read enough to hear what kind of response this Jesus is likely to give. So what do you expect to hear now? Would you guess, "Don't touch me"?

No! Never! It makes no sense. It's bad storytelling. It's suddenly a terrible, different character. You hear the absurdity. "Don't touch me." Like, I'm going to call your name and then stand aloof. Ick. "Don't touch me." Like, after all the spiritual stuff I've just done, I'm on a different plane from you clumsy mortals. Creepy, honestly. Translation matters enormously. Thank God for the language nerds who know Jesus' voice!

Back to reality: Mary falls forward, she grabs his clothes, his hands, his face, his hair. She makes a fool of herself in her belief and disbelief. She hits him with her fists, laughing, dancing, staring, sobbing. Asking his eyes with her eyes, "You!? Really?! How!?" Jesus laughs, and weeps with her, and holds her close and comforts her with THESE words, "Don't cling to me!" Yes, I am here. I, myself. Don't cling to me; you don't HAVE to! I'm not going anywhere! We have some wonderful days ahead before I go back to my Father, but even then I will be with you always in a new way, and I will send the Comforter. He's wonderful; you're going to love him. He'll lead you like I did.

The Greek (in which the Lord chose to record the story) *me mou haptou* is "Don't cling to me!" The expression, obvious if you know who's talking, is one of comfort, of promise, of solidity and stability.

Every time he appears to his people after the resurrection, he makes it very clear that he is flesh and blood and welcomes their physical contact. He makes breakfast on the beach for his boys. He invites Thomas to probe his healing wounds. And so it is with us.

Far from "Don't touch me!," he invites us to the table. To literally taste and see that the Lord is good. We feel the splash of baptismal water. Redemption is being bought back into HIS kingdom, which is a WEDDING FEAST. Expect a physical resurrection and a life of tangible joy.

He says to Mary and to us, "I'm not going anywhere. Hang on as tight as you want, but you don't need to try to keep me here. I did battle for the reward of sitting here with you. *Me mou haptou*; I'll never leave you or forsake you."

Thank you, faithful language nerds. We need you. With a right telling of the story comes a clearer and clearer understanding of just who this Lord is. And then we keep our wits about us as we encounter him in other stories. We allow ourselves to hear who he is, not who we're afraid he might be, or who others have wrongly told us he is.

With Mary in the garden, he is all joyful tears and comfort for his dear grieving friend. Jesus is the full revelation of the Father. This is who God is. He is a real person, a complex, multifaceted, multilayered personality. Not to mention Trinity in Unity and Unity in Trinity. We should expect to be surprised and challenged by what we hear sometimes. Only remember! The Jesus who is so tender toward sweet, faithful Mary, is the same one who can strap his armor on, pick up a sword, and go to war to protect her. Let's look at Isaiah.

When I'm looking for reasons to keep the Lord at arm's length, I love to criticize his behavior in the Old Testament. He does horrible, violent things. Isaiah 30 and 31 describes God destroying the Assyrians. Swooping in and routing them. And God is the good guy? How?

> …every stroke of the appointed staff that the Lord

> lays on [your enemies] will be to the sound of tambourines and harps.[1]

The Assyrians are being shattered to pieces; they're terrified. They're running to their horses, only to be pursued and mown down. Jesus is shattering them. Jesus is mowing them down. And there's music playing! Like, epic movie music—the grand and joyful kind. Why is he so mean and violent? How can he kill people to the triumphant part of the soundtrack?

Here's how: there is a historical narrative to tell here; the Assyrians were a violent empire which rapaciously invaded Northern Israel and slaughtered them, but the label "Assyrian" doesn't only mean an ethnic or political group. "The Assyrian" means the one in your own life, beloved child of God, who lied to you. "The Assyrians" are those who built trust based on nothing so they could get you alone, divided from the world and from the one who desperately loves you, believing yourself beyond rescue. They lie that you are unloved. They lie that you are alone. Abusers do that. Psychopaths do that. You get used to being lied to; you start to ask for comfort that you know is fake. The Israelites can't bear being captives, but they can't imagine release, so they ask the prophet to tell them lies. In your desperation for significance, your religion becomes nothing but (verse 10)

---

[1] Isaiah 30:32 ESV

"Tell us pleasant things! Prophesy illusions!" It's all meaningless, but a momentary lovely fiction is all you've come to expect. It's all you think you deserve.

What do the Assyrians want out of lying to you like this? To dominate you. To devour you, to consume you, to slake their thirst on you. The Assyrians are the abuser who has made his victim hopeless. And life has lost its luster. And the music no longer plays. And you believe you brought it all on yourself. And there's no way out. Think about this abuser. Stop and consider him. Thinking about anyone specifically? How do you feel right now?

I want the prison walls to topple. I want the lights to blaze. I want a giant lion with huge teeth to tear the liars apart and carry you away to safety. I want the hero to be merciless in his rescue. I want to hear music playing when he looks the Assyrians in the eye. He knows what they did. You can't lie to him. Not and get away with it. The liar is cornered.

How does the abuser feel when he's found out? How does the self-reliant and self-justifying feel when his power is taken away? When he realizes he can't get away with his violence and domination? We want the good guy to drag the abuser out of his lair and bring him to account. We want to hear the megaphone blaring, "You're surrounded! Come out with your hands up!" See him blink and flinch and cower when the SWAT team bursts in.

"The Assyrians will be terror-stricken at the voice of the Lord.." Yeah, they will. "And every stroke of the appointed staff that the Lord lays on them will be to the sound of tambourines and harps." And full orchestra. The hero is coming.

The Assyrians are being shattered to pieces; they're terrified. They're running to their horses, only to be pursued and mown down. Jesus is shattering them. Jesus is mowing them down. And there's music playing! Like, epic movie music—the grand and joyful kind. Oh yes. He is violent and beautiful.

Assyrians, you better surrender. Assyrians, you better switch sides and get behind the hero who is bearing down on the ones who also hurt you. And there's music playing. He is coming.

...

So here we have God's texts telling us two massively different kinds of stories. But what if it's the same exact person in both stories? Really sit with that for a second. The Rescuer in Armor told Mary he wasn't going anywhere and gave her time to catch her breath. The tender, protective father roars in to destroy the bad guy. Who is this complex, multifaceted, multilayered personality? The more we read with understanding of who he is, the more what we read comes to life. The more we encounter God, as if he were a real person. Because he is.

And that's what it means to be his sheep that hear his voice. We come to know him, to watch him, to experience him, in the Word and in the world. You'll find yourself saying, "Oh yeah, that sounds like him!" "My sheep hear my voice, and I know them. And they follow me."

Don't miss that middle bit. I am invited to know him as I read his texts, keeping in mind who it is who wrote them, and all the while he is knowing me.

PRACTICE:

Read Mary in the garden (John 20:11–17), and describe Jesus for yourself. Use your imagination. Describe Mary. What does it feel like to weep, and to try to see through your tears? What is Jesus like if he's saying, "You don't have to cling to me. I'm not going anywhere"?

How would it feel if he were saying that to you right now?

Read the Routing of the Assyrians for yourself, in Isaiah 30:27–31:9. If it were Jesus in both places (spoiler: it is), what would be driving his extreme wrath? What could make him so angry at people who had dragged his kids out of their home and into slavery?

How would you feel if you were in prison and saw him break through the walls to come get you?

9

DOES GOD WANT TO BE NEAR ME?

Liv

Moses had to take off his shoes at the burning bush. The men who reached out to stabilize the Ark of the Covenant fell down dead. Doesn't this mean God needs to be separated from me? That his natural state is to be far away?

After all, a quick explanation of the Gospel usually starts with something like "God cannot abide sin" or "God cannot stand to be in the presence of evil." I'm supposed to understand that I am too evil for God to be near me, right? I'm some kind of gross bug, or a nasty smell.

Distance seems to be the theme between me and God. Let's look at Isaiah 65:5: "Keep to yourself, do not come near me, for I am too holy for you."

Sit with that for a second. Read it again several times.

What is the facial expression of the speaker? What is the speaker wearing? What are the hands doing?

And what is the posture of the one who must "keep to themselves"? What should they do while they're "not coming near"? What would happen if they came near to that which was "too holy for them"?

"Keep to yourself, do not come near me, for I am too holy for you."

Listen to this from Luke 8. Jesus was met with "a man who had demons. For a long time he had worn no clothes, and he had not lived in a house, but among the tombs. When he saw Jesus, he cried out and fell down before him and said with a loud voice, 'What have you to do with me, Jesus, Son of the Most High God? I beg you not to torment me!'"

This demon-possessed man then said one of the most chilling things we hear a demon say in the New Testament. This man responds to Jesus' question, "What is your name?," with "Legion" (chills).

And listen. Notice that Jesus doesn't hang back. It is THIS man who tells Jesus to keep his distance. This man, full of demons, says God should not come near. Why? What would Jesus do to him? What cruelty had this tormented man suffered at Jesus' hands? Jesus had only commanded the unclean spirit to come out of the man.

But Legion itself is not wrong. Jesus means all kinds of hurt to Legion. It has been met in battle by the Lord of Angelic Armies, the King of Heaven. Legion is about to be toast. Well, as we know, it does become quite a lot of bacon.

Let me repeat. Who says, "Keep to yourself, do not come near!"? It's not Jesus. It is this poor man, full of demons. This man filled with lies and pain and hopelessness. This naked, lonely man.

Even people who love Jesus explain that he should keep his distance from them. John the Baptizer said, "I should be baptized by you, and do you come to me??" Peter said to him, "Never Lord! You will never wash my feet!" The voice of sinful humanity cries out, "Stay away, Lord! Keep to yourself! Do not come near!" Whether we think we are too special for God (either too clean or too dirty) or whether we know he comes with healing in his wings, and being whole scares the shit out of us, we would hold him off with false piety or straight rebellion. "Keep to yourself! Sit quietly like a good little god. Fold your hands and close your eyes and wait for me to direct you."

But it is not in the Lord's nature to stay away. This standoffishness is humanity's treatment of the Lord. WE cry out "stay away." The Lion and the Lamb cry, "Behold, I am coming soon." "Underneath are the Everlasting Arms." "I am with you always." "I in them and they in me, and we in You," like we've been caught up into the inner workings of the Holy Trinity himself! Which we have, dear ones. The incarnation of our Lord brings humanity up into God. Goodness and Mercy, in person, shall pursue us all the days of our lives.

We imagine it is God's nature to hold us off, but we are

(yet again) remaking God in OUR own image. We are the ones who say, "don't come near!" He says, standing in the Garden, "Adam! Where are you?" He says, standing in the Garden on Resurrection Morning, "Mary!" He will say, on Resurrection Day, "Come to me, all who are weary and heavy laden and I will give your soul and body real rest. I have called you by name; you are mine." And he gives us the grace to say, with Mary, "Master!" and to fall into his everlasting arms.

Let's hear the full context of the speech I quoted briefly above from Isaiah:

> "I was ready to be sought by those who did not ask for me; I was ready to be found by those who did not seek me. I said, 'Here am I, here am I,' to a nation that was not called by my name. I spread out my hands all the day to a rebellious people, who walk in a way that is not good, following their own devices; a people who provoke me to my face continually, sacrificing in gardens and making offerings on bricks; who sit in tombs, and spend the night in secret places; who eat pig's flesh, and broth of tainted meat is in their vessels; who say, 'Keep to yourself, do not come near me, for I am too holy for you.'"[1]

It is we, poor tormented ones, filled with lies and pain

---

[1] Isaiah 65:1-5 ESV

and hopelessness. We naked, lonely souls who tell him to have nothing to do with us. He should keep his distance; he should never find me or wash my feet. Whether we feel we are too holy, too independent, or too corrupt, depraved, a lost cause—surely he wants to stay away. To hide from me.

But it was Adam who hid. The Lord did not hide. He didn't keep to himself. He came near. "Adam, where are you?"

Look back to your first response to Isaiah 65:5. Maybe you thought it was the Lord speaking? Sitting on a cold white throne in judge's robes, ordering some little human to lower their eyes? Requiring some little human to cower in fear and yet, perversely, to love him? It changes everything when we realize that it's me speaking! I'm telling God to hang back, not to presume my good favor. Because I don't need him. I'm set apart, special, holy.

Look with pity on the little human striking whatever pose you imagined during the exercise. The little human is telling God to cower, to shrink back, to retreat. It sounds like the kid who knows they've done wrong, scared on the inside but defiant on the outside. Chin stuck out, angry tears in his eyes, but inwardly desperate for his good parent to overcome his resistance and hold him close. The flip side of the accusation "You don't care about me!!" is "Please be near me!!"

Thank God he is not deterred by our resistance. He refuses to keep to himself. He will come near. It is who he is.

And when he does, we discover an amazing truth: I am near to God. His full holiness, life, strength and love is not dangerous to me. I belong here—close.

And when I'm where I belong, receiving the presence of the Lord, amazing things happen.

What happened when Legion was driven out of the man? They found him dressed and in his right mind, at the feet of Jesus.

And John the Baptist found the Messiah,

and Peter found his Purifier,

and Adam found his Rescuer

and Mary found her dear Lord and Teacher.

He is near. Hear his voice, watch his hands, see his expression, when the Lord of Heaven, the Commander of the Angelic Armies says, "I am here to do my Father's will. Let the little children come to me, and do not hinder them. The kingdom is theirs; I am theirs; everything is theirs since I have come near."

So who am I, really? May I share my personal self-image (when I'm consenting to the truth) with you?

I am a child held by my good Father while I push against his chest. Sometimes I push and squirm until I'm hot and sweaty because I want to throw myself out of his arms, but he holds me tight, which is what I actually want. Sometimes I push because I want to know he's still there. Sometimes I just push like a kitten affectionately kneading its mother. Pushing makes him familiar to me because I feel him more and more as I resist him from up close. It's how I learn. Infants press their faces against your neck, toddlers bonk their foreheads against yours; young kids absent-mindedly lean against their mother; teens lay their heads briefly on mom's shoulder. It's big: this brief contact is consent to the loving presence of their parent.

I hear his word, watch how he works in people's lives, receive all his gifts, and as my trust grows, I admit that he is already near. I can never be too bad or too holy to hold him off. I am as near to him as that squirmy child, or Adam walking with the Lord in the garden in the cool of the day.

Who am I? I am the Beloved. You might try saying it aloud, "I am near him. I am the Beloved."

10

HOW?

Brandon

Allow me to summarize where we are so far. I am God's beloved. To him, I'm worth everything. He is driven by compassion to be with me always. What wonderful news! I'm not alone in this world! If God is with me, who or what can truly harm me? Nothing.

When I'm confident and secure in God's loving presence, I'm also free. Free to offer compassion and presence to others. It's just like we said at the beginning, when I know who Jesus really is, I can trust him. I'm welcomed "home" into his loving embrace, and I then can extend that embrace to others.

But at this point someone always, rightly, asks, "Okay, sure, I believe that's true, but how do I *feel* like it's true?"

I can relate! Mere information *about* God does very little to change me. I need to experience God's loving presence in order to trust him. Without that, the information alone is likely to breed cognitive dissonance and shame. At least that's my experience. I have mentally assented to these truths about God for as long as I can remember, but I have rarely felt the overwhelming peace and security that I think I *should* feel as a result. What am I doing wrong? Did I sleep through the Sunday School class that everyone else seems to have heard?

I want to feel like God loves me, like I'm forgiven, like I'm safe, all the time. But no matter what I do, I always slip back into fear, doubt, and anxiety. Sure, today I might feel pretty good, but tomorrow the car breaks down, and there's no money in my account, and I behave like I've never trusted God at all. Today I'm able to believe that I'm God's beloved, but tomorrow I embarrass myself at work, or return to that old sin, and immediately I'm convinced God must hate me, and I'm total trash. Today I'm able to believe God is enough, but tomorrow I'm tired, or scared, or hurt, and God doesn't feel close or safe. What gives?!

What must I do to feel better? How do I trust God perfectly all the time?

I don't.

Give up.

Admit defeat.

That's the answer.

That's the big secret.

That's the real answer to life, the universe, and everything.[1]

I'll bet that's not the answer you were expecting. I know it's not the answer that I want to hear. I want a nicely laid-out series of steps, a few ultra-special spiritual practices, a magical insight, the correct doctrinal system, anything! Just tell me what to do so that I can always feel like I'm safe and significant and never doubt God, and I'll do it!

But I don't have any of those things. Worse still, anyone who claims to have THE ANSWER is selling you snake oil. Because any answer that says, "Just do this…" or "just read this…" or "just remember this…" turns my relationship with God into a transaction. *You* do this… and *then* God will do this…. It's the illusion of control. It subtly puts me in God's place.

Let me see if I can explain.

The first step in the 12 steps of Alcoholics Anonymous is to admit utter defeat. It's to admit that I'm utterly powerless over my addiction and that *I need help*. The Big Book says it best:

> Most people try to live by self-propulsion. Each person is like an actor who wants to run the whole show; is forever trying to arrange the lights, the ballet, the scenery and the rest of the players in his own way…. Is he not a victim of the delusion that he can wrest

---

[1] This last one's a joke. For the uninitiated, it's a silly reference to *The Hitchhiker's Guide to the Galaxy* by Douglas Adams. If you don't get it, don't worry about it!

> satisfaction and happiness out of this world if he only manages well?...
>
> **This is the how and why of it. First of all, we had to quit playing God. It didn't work. Next, we decided that hereafter in this drama of life, God was going to be our Director. He is the Principal; we are His agents. He is the Father, and we are His children.** Most good ideas are simple, and this concept was the keystone of the new and triumphant arch through which we passed to freedom.[2]

This is The Answer. This is the pivot point on which everything hinges, the keystone in the arch, the foundation on which everything rests. This admission of complete defeat—of complete powerlessness to manage my own life, to "figure out" how to feel better—is the first step of *faith*.

WHAT IS FAITH?

"Faith" is extraordinarily risky to analyze and describe. Wars have been fought over its precise theological meaning. Is it a choice or not? Is it belief with my head or trust with my heart? Is it something I do, or something I *don't* do? Is it a meritorious work or a gift of grace?

Instead of defining faith I prefer to embrace the paradoxical way we experience it. And for me, the picture that sums that experience up is a roller coaster.

---

[2] *The Big Book of Alcoholics Anonymous,* 60

Trusting God feels like that moment of hesitation right at the top of the first hill before the roller coaster drops. Right then I both have a choice and don't have a choice. I *am* going down that hill. There's nothing I can do about it. It's simply the reality of the situation. But I can choose to accept my fate or not. I can consent to reality or not.

Choosing to resist doesn't change anything, except my experience of the ride. I'm still going down that hill and through all the rest of it, but I'll close my eyes, tighten all my muscles, and fight every bump and turn. And I won't be able to see things as they really are.

Choosing, instead, to abandon myself to the roller coaster's care by literally letting go of the safety bar and throwing my hands in the air doesn't change the reality either. But it does allow me to notice just how safe I am. How awesome the roller coaster is. How many other people are with me on the ride. Don't get me wrong, it's still a wild and scary ride, but with just a little bit of faith, I can experience it a bit differently. Maybe even as fun.

I'm not saying that you can experience life as always fun. (All analogies break down eventually.) What I am saying is that *faith* is not something I do; it's something I don't do. It's something I let happen to me.

This is the answer I've been looking for. How do I experience God as massively good? How do I feel his unconditional love for me? How do I feel safe in his forgiving, powerful arms?

Well, that's a little bit like asking, "How do I enjoy a

roller coaster ride?" As long as I'm trying really hard, expending a lot of effort, resisting the plunge, I can't enjoy it. The answer is to stop trying so hard. To let go.

Throw my hands up and give into reality. Let it be true that God is love. Let it be true that Jesus is a good shepherd and that I'm safe even when the shadow of death hovers over me. I'm not saying this is easy, or that it's the magic answer that will make you feel better. What I am saying is that those things are already true. And faith is consent to reality. Faith is abandoning myself to God and letting him do *whatever* he wants to do with me because he is good.

BUT HOW!

I know, I know! It makes no sense. What are the steps? What process do I go through to get myself to the point of letting go? I want to abandon myself to God; I want to believe that God is good, that he forgives me, that he *likes* me, but I can't. It's too hard. It's too scary.

I understand. I feel that too. But I have to be honest. If you are asking that question right now, it's more than likely a disingenuous question. You're like a small child standing on the edge of the pool looking down at your daddy holding up his hands.

"Jump, Buddy! I promise, I'll catch you!" he says. And you and I stand there asking, "But *how* do I do that?"

The answer is obvious. JUMP!

There is no "how." There is only the leap. Or, perhaps better the *fall,* because faith is not a jump into God's hands, it's a fall off the end of our rope, giving up of trying to maintain my balance on the tightrope, a dropping of the illusion that I can fly.

Falling is scary! And I ask, "What do I have to do to make this not scary? Explain it to me; make it easy!"

Sorry. That's not possible. Jumping into the pool or falling into God's hands feels scary. There's no way around it. The only thing for it is to do it.

This is the only real "action" any of us ever does in life. We stop trying so hard to keep our balance and we just… fall.

Here is the deep secret of Christian faith: take the leap once, drop off whatever rope you're clinging to just once, let Jesus catch you just once, and you'll experience that he is there. The next time will be much easier. I promise!

But what does it feel like? What does God's loving presence feel like? I don't know—whatever you feel like *right now*, because God is already present. God does already love you. God is already compassionately with you.

Whether you feel something or nothing, it doesn't change the reality that God loves you and is with you. And with just a little bit of faith, you can, sometimes, notice it.

A LITTLE REPRIEVE, OR, WHERE I ACTUALLY TELL YOU HOW TO DO IT

Now, ironically, let me tell you exactly how to do this. There are two steps, which I have adapted from the 12 steps of AA:

First, I must admit that I'm powerless—that I cannot, and never could, manage my own life.

Second, I come to believe that God is good and only he can manage my life and restore me, so I turn my will and my life over to his care.

Let's unpack that. First, I must admit that I'm powerless—that I cannot, and never could, manage my own life. That I need help. This actually doesn't require any faith, only honesty. Life pushes us all to the brink. I'm not saying it's easy to admit my powerlessness. I'd much rather ignore this truth, run from it, or distract myself from it, but then again, in another way it's the easiest thing in the world to admit. Just ask yourself, how are your efforts to get everything in your life under control working out for you?

Second, I need to come to believe that God is actually good. That he is actually good *for me*. That he actually wants to rescue and help me. This is a big leap of (or fall into) faith. And there's nothing for it. It's scary! It feels like a leap into a bottomless pit. Our experience of the world is that nothing and no one is truly trustworthy, so why would I trust God?

I need help. I need to experience love. I need some assurance that God will catch me. Some felt sense that God is actually good. Otherwise, the leap really is foolish. There's absolutely no sense in leaping into a pit of deadly snakes.

This is why hospitality is a central theme of this book. Hospitality is where I get a taste of God's goodness through another person. Hospitality gives the skeptic a taste of God's authentic love. It gives the doubter a glimpse of God's good will. It gives the fearful a ray of hope that God might actually care. It makes the leap a little bit easier. If it's possible that another broken human would accept me, forgive me, love me some of the time, then it's possible that there is a Perfect Person who will do it all of the time.

We don't have to jump alone. We don't have to fall alone. We have help. Then—when we leap into Papa's strong arms—we learn that God is actually present. That he is actually good. Our heads don't go under water! The next time I'm asked to leap, it's just a little bit easier. And the next time it's a little bit easier still.

It never becomes, you know, *easy!* There's always that anxiety just before I leap, *maybe this time God won't catch me!* But when you *know* God is good, when you have been "hugged" by God, it doesn't feel quite as impossible to take that final step and turn my will and life over to his care.

SPIRITUAL PRACTICES

This "leap of faith" or "fall into grace" is what makes any practice "spiritual" in the true, Christian sense.

Take fasting for example. Fasting has become trendy. The spiritual-but-not-religious-types do it to cleanse themselves. The health-conscious types do it to encourage gut health. There are even apps to help you do it to lose weight.

But the true spiritual practice of fasting is practice in trusting God. I choose to forgo a meal or two, experience hunger—experience my helplessness in a small way—and then trust God to sustain me. With each hunger pang I might recite some words from Scripture as a prayer of consent. For example:

- "It is written: Man must not live on bread alone but on every word that comes from the mouth of God."[3]
- "Don't worry, saying, 'What will we eat?' or 'What will we drink?' or 'What will we wear?' For the Gentiles eagerly seek all these things, and your Heavenly Father knows that you need them. But seek first the kingdom of God and his righteousness, and all these things will be provided for you."[4]

I'm not going to test God or anything, demanding that he miraculously provide manna from Heaven, but I am going to practice experiencing need, and noticing all the ways he has sustained and presently does sustain me.

Consider the practices of solitude, silence, and stillness. These, the foundations of Christian spiritual practice, are each a kind of withdrawing or fasting. In each of these we can experience our need, our limitedness and dependence, and practice trusting God to be our sustenance.

In all cases, Christian spiritual practices are doing one thing: practicing leaping (or falling) into God's loving arms. We are abandoning ourselves to God. Surrendering our self-will. We are practicing doing nothing. That is, we are practicing faith.

In his classic work *Abandonment to Divine Providence,* Jean-Pierre de Caussade says it beautifully:

---

[3] Matthew 4:4 CSB
[4] Matthew 6:31-33 CSB

> Do not ask me for the secret of finding this treasure [of sanctity]. There is no secret. This treasure is everywhere. It is offered to us at every moment and in every place. All things, both friendly and hostile, pour it out freely and make it pervade every faculty of body and soul, right to the depths of our hearts. We have only to open our mouths and they will be filled. Divine activity floods the whole universe; it pervades all things and flows over them. Wherever they are, it is there: it precedes, accompanies, and follows them. We have but to allow ourselves to be carried forward on the crest of its waves… This is the spirituality of all ages and all states of life which assuredly cannot be made holy in a nobler, more wonderful, and easier manner than by simply making use of what God, the supreme director of souls, gives them to do or suffer at each moment.[5]

Christian spiritual practices are not feats of will. They are not saint-making workout routines. They are instead waving the white flag of surrender. They are laying down our arms. They are trust-falls into the infinite compassion of Jesus.

And practice makes perfect. Or, in this fallen world where perfection is impossible, practice makes surrender easier the next time.

---

[5] Trans. Dennis Billy. Classics with Commentary. Ave Maria Press 2010. 28-29

AND THEN?

And then, slowly, as I practice, I become more and more able to extend hospitality to others. Again, never perfectly, but just a little bit more freely, more genuinely. As I increasingly experience the compassionate presence of God, I can increasingly drop my defenses against other people and let them in.

Over the next few chapters we are going to explore a few other spiritual practices that we have found to be central in our lives. Things that we have found to be very powerful in helping us learn to trust God and become more hospitable. It starts with an encouragement to be vulnerable.

11

BEING VULNERABLE

Brandon

My family loves watching reality survival shows. One of our favorites is "ALONE." There are no camera crews, no gimmicks, just individual men and women dropped off in extremely remote places and left to survive with limited gear. It's a competition of who can last the longest. The last person standing wins an absurd amount of money. The longest survivor to date? One hundred days.

No matter how skilled the survivalist, they all give up eventually. The one thing that gets them all is in the name of the show. They are *alone*. Eventually they can't find enough food, or water, or the emotional strain becomes too much.

We are vulnerable by nature. It's part of what it means

to have a physical body. We can be hurt; we depend on things and people outside of us to live. We are limited. We are mortal.

Sometimes it feels as if it would be better if we weren't vulnerable, but to cease to be vulnerable would mean to stop being human. We can't do that without destroying ourselves.

But we're not just vulnerable physically. We are also vulnerable emotionally and spiritually. We need secure relationships where we can be vulnerable, physically and emotionally. We need to be able to be vulnerable and be cared for in our vulnerability. It's a basic human need; even more basic than my need for food and shelter. As babies and children, having food and shelter depends on having people who care about us. We would literally die if we were left alone. And that's still true for us adults, both physically and emotionally. Think about it: how long could you survive alone in the woods?

Please note, this is a *feature* of being human, *not* a bug. We were created to live in family, in community. Our vulnerability is a good consequence of being made to be social. We were designed with physical, emotional, and spiritual needs– created to share those needs with others. It's what allows us to connect. It's how we receive, and give, love.

PLEASE, FIND PLACES WHERE YOU CAN BE VULNERABLE

Being vulnerable—in safe relationships—means being able to let my guard down. It means letting others know what

I'm really like behind my everyday mask.

When I drop my defenses and find that I am cared for, that I'm wanted, I feel valued. I feel safe. I'm not alone in this world. I don't have to fend for myself. I have support. I *need* this. Almost more than I need food, water, or shelter. (It's a prerequisite for these!)

Being rejected is terrifying because it means I'm alone, unprotected. Being unwanted feels like an existential threat because it *is* an existential threat. No one has all the resources they need to survive alone for long. Without people who care about me, I'm in real danger. We all desperately need secure relationships where we can experience the joy of being known, accepted and loved.

I can remember many times when I really experienced that kind of acceptance. They are like oases in the desert of life. One was when, as an adult, I cried with my head in a friend's lap. We were sitting on an old couch in his garage; he was listening to me talk about a deep pain in my life. He didn't say much; he just made it clear that it was safe to express the grief I was carrying. When I fell apart, sobbing like a baby, he reached out to put his arm around my shoulders, and I fell over weeping.

It's one of my proudest moments. I'm not kidding! I look back at that time and see my courage. I dropped all my defenses and took a "leap" of faith to trust my friend. Do you know how much courage it takes for a grown man to weep like a baby in the presence of another man? A LOT! The reward, feeling cared for, is worth the risk!

I also feel deeply accepted when one of Liv's and my

favorite love songs plays on Spotify. I won't scandalize you with all the lyrics, but the chorus goes like this: "Because I've seen you / And I know you / And I'm not going anywhere."

When this song plays, it doesn't matter what we're doing, we both stop, look into each other's eyes and sing with everything we've got. We've been through *a lot* together. She *knows* me—good and bad—and she isn't going anywhere.

I'm not alone. People know me and accept me. I'm enough. I'm loved.

How do you feel right now? Afraid? Jealous? Maybe you have some secure relationships in your life where this deep need to be wanted is met, so you feel grateful?

I hope it's the last one. I hope you have many secure places and relationships in your life. But if not, and you're feeling a little bit afraid, please take a moment to pause and feel beneath that fear. What are you afraid of? I've been there, and I'm willing to bet it's a fear (which I have shared) that you are uniquely disgusting. That if anyone knew the "real you" they would throw you away and leave you *alone.*

I know that feeling too. You are not crazy. You are not the only one. Go back and revisit our earlier chapters about how Jesus sees you.

He says you are enough for him. He knows your frailty, your weakness, even your sin, and he isn't disgusted. He's attracted. Like an ocean of love, the deeper the abyss in my soul the faster he rushes in. You are not too burdensome or too needy or too dumb. Jesus sees you, and knows you, and he's not going anywhere. He loves you as his very own son or daughter. You will never be truly *alone!*

Still, I know that for many these are just words. It's a nice sentiment, but where's the reality?

The incarnate grace of hospitality. Other human beings physically welcoming us into their spaces and explicitly telling us that we are valuable to them. That they care about us. We need Jesus' love to be enfleshed. In plain language, we need other human beings to give us little tastes, little experiences, of Jesus' unconditional approval and love of us. Hospitality preaches the gospel.

I implore you to seek out people with whom you can be vulnerable! Communities where you can feel and hear that you are welcome, known, and cared for. You need that more than anything.

WHERE?

There are several ways you can find such places. One is obviously spiritual direction or a retreat with Signpost Inn Ministries. Another is with a good therapist. Another is with a good church community and/or small group. Or a support group for whatever your issues are (they exist for almost everything now!).

Whatever, or however, you can get connected with another human being who can hear what's really going on in your life, and look you in the eyes and say, "You are loved; you are enough. I see you and care about you." You need it.

And then, create those places for others!

In ancient Hebrew culture, being hospitable was required by God's law. A host would go out and meet a stranger on his way. He welcomed the guest, fed him and cared for his basic needs and those of his animals before even asking his name or the purpose of travels. The host brought him into his home, offered him a place to stay, and took responsibility for his personal safety. Then, upon departure, the host would travel some distance with the sojourner and ensure he had everything he needed for his journey.

God's reasoning for all this? "For you were strangers in the land of Egypt."[1] The Israelites knew what it was like to be vulnerable. They had been cared for, then enslaved, and finally rescued and welcomed into a new home. The Israelites knew what it was like to be alone and then cared for.

So do we. All of us have experienced the terrifying threat of being rejected. Many of us have also experienced the glorious security of being welcomed, so we have the responsibility and privilege to care about others as Christ has cared about us.

THE FIRST PRINCIPLE OF HOSPITALITY

Notice the principle at work in the ancient Hebrew practice of hospitality. The host went out to the stranger and met him on his way. He asked no questions until the stranger's needs had been met. It's an intentional move of vulnerability on the host's part. The host willingly exposes himself to

---

[1] Leviticus 19:34 ESV

potential harm by leaving the safety of his home and offering care before he knows anything about the stranger.

Every culture has a version of this. In its simplest and least vulnerable form, it's a handshake. Or, in my martial arts training, I was taught to bow and grip one fist in the palm of my other hand. Both traditions are a form of "showing your hands" so the other can see you don't have a weapon. They are mild ways of dropping your own guard so the other person can drop theirs. We create safety for others to be vulnerable by being appropriately vulnerable first.

This is the first job of any host desiring to offer Christian hospitality. I want to make you feel comfortable, safe, and that means being the first one to be a little bit vulnerable. As we discuss the practical aspects of hospitality, I hope you'll see the many ways you can appropriately do this. For now, here are a few little examples.

When I meet a new directee for spiritual direction I often tell them just a little bit of my own spiritual journey. Without going into detail, I let people know that I've been through severe family tragedy and have struggled with intense anxiety. Sometimes, if they ask, I'll give a bit more detail. For example, I will let them know that I have had such severe panic attacks that I've curled up into the fetal position for hours in my closet, trying to hide from the world. These are past struggles, things I'm not currently struggling with, so they don't feel like I'm asking for help, but they do tell you about some of my weaknesses and vulnerabilities.

I have to be careful not to overshare. That would be manipulative. Instead, I'm giving folks a small peek behind my polite mask. I'm human, just like you, and I've trusted you with an important part of my life's story. You can trust me too.

Another, perhaps silly example, but one that I find effective, is to answer the question, "How are you?" honestly. I like being a greeter at church, and in my previous ministry work I greeted parents dropping their children off at camp every week of every summer. In both cases it's *sometimes* helpful to answer the question, "How are you?" with a *little* more honesty than, "I'm good, how are you!"

I might smile and say, "Ah, that's a complicated question, do you want the short answer or the long one?" If they say they want the long answer I give a few more honest details about my life. For example, I might say, "Well, honestly, my baby puked all over my good shirt this morning" (a frequent occurrence during my younger days), "so I had to do an entire load of laundry before breakfast this morning. I'm pretty frazzled!" or "Well, honestly, I got out of the house late today and totally forgot my computer bag until I got here. I had to rush home and get it and rush back here, so I'm feeling a little bit harried."

Again, remember that all of this is context and person-specific. Appropriate vulnerability in one situation is inappropriate oversharing in another. This takes some discernment and practice. Go slowly at first, feel your way forward carefully. You're not trying to manipulate; you're just trying to give a little bit of yourself so that the other person feels comfortable giving a little bit of themselves.

That's the first principle of hospitality: being vulnerable makes it safe for others to be vulnerable, and we all desperately need places where it is safe to be vulnerable.

12

PRAYER

Brandon

Prayer is a Christian practice of receiving God's hospitality—his loving presence—on a continual basis. It's how I accept God's provisions that sustain me on my long passage in this world that is not my home. Prayer is being with God, and trusting that God wants to be with me. Through prayer I learn to be vulnerable and safe with God. Then I can drop my defenses around others and be hospitable towards them.

Let me set one thing straight right away. There is no right way to pray. It's tempting when talking about prayer to jump straight to discussing methods, as if prayer is a skill to be mastered like playing the piano or a sport. But the moment we do that we set ourselves up for failure.

Prayer does require discipline, but it's not a discipline to be mastered. Rather, as Henri Nouwen explains, "in the spiritual life, the word discipline means 'the effort to create some space in which God can act.'"[1]

The truth is, the only way we can fail in prayer is to not pray. That's because "prayer" is just a fancy term for conversation with God. Just like normal conversation with others, there is no right way or special technique. We just talk.

Sure, I speak differently in different situations. Quietly in a library for example, or loudly at a baseball game. I can learn some conversational skills which make me a better conversational partner, but conversation is not a competitive game or a battle (though I know we often engage it those ways). At its best, conversation is more like a dance. A lovely, collaborative way of being with another person and enjoying their company.[2]

In the same way, our conversation with God can take different forms depending on the situation. More formal in church, more informal and personal when alone. We can have angry conversations with God, grateful conversations, fearful conversations, and all the rest. But there is one way that specifically Christian prayer differs from normal conversation: our prayer is always a *response* to God.

Jesus is always the one who speaks—who loves—first. Prayer is never me talking into a void or babbling a bunch

---

[1] "Moving from solitude to community to ministry: Jesus established the true order for spiritual work" Published in *Leadership* 16, no. 2 (spring 1995): 80-87

[2] See my book *Changing the Conversation: How to dance instead of fight in everyday conversation* for a much more in-depth exploration of this.

of holy-sounding words hoping God will notice and approve. No, the fundamental truth of Christian prayer is that Jesus loves me, that he is always directly and personally attending to me, that he has made himself present to me, *first*.

I don't need to get God's attention. I already have it. I don't need to ask God to be present. He already is. My prayer begins by noticing and attending to God who is already with me. Prayer begins when I *respond* to God's personal, interested, and loving presence that is always with me.

Prayer is not something I do for God. It's my response to all that God is already doing for *me*. Prayer is hearing Jesus say, "I love you!" and then me saying back to God, "I love you, too."

Many people are afraid they might mess their praying up. But how can I mess up responding to God who is saying, "I love you!"? There's only one way. To refuse to respond. To ignore him. That means *any* prayer is a good prayer, because at least we're acknowledging God's presence and talking to him!

This fear often leads to unrealistic ideals about the amount of time or kind of prayer we *should* be doing. I may think, for example, "I really should get up at 5 am every morning and spend an hour reading my Bible and fervently praying," or "I have to pray according to the right formula!" I end up treating God like a spiritual gas station. I go to the "pump" to try and purchase God's energy and support with my time and effort.

But remember, prayer is a *response* to God's presence and

support. The first step in prayer is to attend to God who is always with me and for me. I don't need to ask for what I already have—and I certainly don't need to purchase it—but I may need to consent to it.

The word "consent" makes a lot of sense to me. Consenting is something I do with my heart more than my mind. It's an internal movement by which I "give in" to reality. Just like I don't need to ask gravity to hold me securely to the earth, but I may need to notice it and consent to it as being a reality, I also don't need to ask God to be present with me or to love me, but I may need to consent to the fact that he is and does.

You may prefer a different word: surrender, trust, abandon, let go. These all capture the same idea of ceasing to resist the unalterable reality of God's presence and love for you.

The first step in all prayer is to notice and attend to God's real and loving presence. The second step is a grateful surrender, acceptance, or *consent* to that reality.

May I invite you to try it right now? Pause for a few moments and quietly attend to God's love. Before doing anything else, before saying anything, simply take a few moments to accept—to consent to—the reality of God's presence and love.

This needn't be a dramatic or mystical experience. It can be as simple as taking three or four deep breaths and noticing how good it feels to fill your lungs with air. Each breath fills your body with life; each breath is the Spirit of God filling you with *his* breath of life. With each breath let your body relax into the reality that God is with you, and for you. With each breath sink deeper into the reality that "in him we live and move and have our being."[3]

It could be as simple as sitting still. The simple act of sitting down can be a huge act of consent to God's love and care for you. For just a few moments you don't have to manage all the details. Your tasks can wait. Your worries can wait. By sitting down and taking a moment, you can say with your body, "Yes, Lord. You care for me; I can take a moment to rest."

What about asking God for things? Is it wrong to ask God for things? Absolutely not! In fact, when I ask God for things I am worshiping God as *my* God. I am consenting to his providential care.

When I bring all my wants and needs to God, I'm doing exactly what Jesus told me to do. I am going to God like a little child in total dependence and saying, "Yes, Jesus, you are good, and only you know and can fill my true needs… and please may I have a candy bar?"

When I ask God for things, I am acknowledging God's love and presence, surrendering to God's goodness and care. I am putting my life into his hands. I am worshiping God as my *God*. I'm trusting him.

When Jesus taught his disciples how to pray, he said, in effect, "face God (acknowledge his presence), call on him as your Father (consent to his love), and then ask him to care for your life, give you your daily bread, and forgive your

---
[3] Acts 17:28 CSB

sins (trust him!)."

Prayer is the water and fertilizer for faith. It's how we practice complete reliance on God and surrender to his good will. Of course it doesn't happen overnight; it grows slowly over time. Just as a tiny seed grows into a great big tree that can support our entire lives and produce magnificent fruit. What matters most is not *how* we practice prayer, but that we *don't stop* practicing it.

This doesn't mean we need to be always talking! Remember, prayer begins with God attending to me. Thus, when Paul instructs us to "pray without ceasing" he is not encouraging us to a continual output of words and effort, but to a continuous posture of receptivity.[4]

PRACTICE

Here are a few practical tips. Talk to God out loud, as if he's right there in the room with you—because he is. Take a walk, or drive, or go have coffee with God. It may feel odd at first, talking aloud to an invisible person who normally doesn't talk back to us audibly. But it's a great way to put your theological money where your mouth is.

You believe that God is really present with you, and really cares. Talk to him that way. When you are done talking, and the silence settles in, imagine Jesus waiting to hear if you have more to say. He's not refusing to talk to you; he's making space for you to really feel understood.

If you have more to say, say it. Take as long as you like.

---

[4] 1 Thessalonians 5:17

When you're done, thank him for listening to you. For loving you enough to spend as much time with you as you need.

Say, "Yes, Father, I accept that you love life and breath and all your gifts into me. Yes, Jesus, my brother, you do. Yes, Holy Spirit, you do. I love you too."[5]

Pray the following prayer of self-abandonment to God written by Jean Pierre de Caussade:

> Father, I abandon myself into your hands; do with me what you will. Whatever you may do, I thank you: I am ready for all, I accept all. Let only your will be done in me, and in all your creatures. I wish no more than this, O Lord. Into your hands I commend my soul; I offer it to you with all the love of my heart, for I love you Lord, and so need to give myself, to surrender myself into your hands, without reserve, and with boundless confidence, I consent to your divine presence and action in my life, for you are my Father.

---

[5] This quote is from a beautiful article written by Armand M. Nigro, S.J. This chapter is heavily indebted to this article which you can read here: https://manresa-canada.ca/blog/2017/07/12/a-personal-response-to-gods-presence/

13

CHURCH

Brandon

A few chapters back I claimed that mere information about God doesn't change me. Gathering and memorizing facts about God does little to change how I feel about him—does little to change my heart towards him. I need *embodied* experiences of God's love, God's hospitality, to feel safe to be vulnerable with him. I'd like to unpack this idea more here, as we discuss the crucial role church plays in helping us become hospitable oases for others.

Let's begin at the beginning. The modern psychological study of attachment has shown that our early experiences with caregivers have a huge influence on our ability to develop secure emotional bonds with others, including God, throughout our lives.

If we had parents who mostly responded to our needs and presence with love and delight, we developed secure emotional bonds with them. We felt loved and safe and could therefore experiment and grow more healthily. We came to expect that relationships can be safe and secure, so we are more likely to find and develop good relationships with others in adulthood.

If our parents were more often distant, uncaring, or abusive, we grew up feeling unwanted and unsafe. This leads to unhealthy patterns of relating later in life. Some people isolate and avoid difficult relationships. Others anxiously fixate on relationships, and unhealthily seek constant approval. Lots of us do a combination of both.

The common thread is that our early relationships with our parents were not secure. We could not expect to receive the care and love we desperately need, so we have learned not to expect security in any relationship, including our relationship with God.

Here's the real kicker: because many of these powerful formative experiences with our parents happened before our brains developed any linguistic or analytical abilities, our memories and learned responses are mostly implicit. They live below the level of consciousness and inhabit our emotions and instinctive physical responses. We automatically engage and respond to relationships with our unhealthy attachment strategies, no thinking necessary.

This creates the possibility of severe cognitive dissonance in our experiences with God. I can know that God loves me. I can answer questions about God's love and goodness correctly on any theological quiz, but if I do not have embodied experience with God's love for me, God feels uncertain or even dangerous. What my head knows and my heart feels conflict.

According to what I "know," I *should* experience God as safe and loving. But my actual experience is very different. God is not safe nor interested in me. I avoid him or pander to him or confusedly do both. I am likely to feel that something is uniquely wrong with me. I *should* feel that God loves me, but I don't, so something must be wrong with me or the way I'm doing this "Christian thing."

More Bible verses or pat theological answers just dig the hole deeper. I feel dumb. "This seems to work for everyone else; am I the only one who doesn't get it?" Or I feel uniquely unlovable. "Everyone else seems to feel God's love; he must just hate me."

Instead of more information about theology, I need actual experiences of being loved and accepted by God. I need to feel his love for me. I need to receive grace and forgiveness in concrete—embodied—ways.

How? One answer is church. That's one place where Jesus can meet me directly, even physically.

I know that church is a difficult topic for many. Many of us have been hurt by bad churches and bad leaders. If that's you, I'm sorry! Seriously, I acknowledge my own part as a member of God's church in not stopping whatever it was from happening to you. You deserved something better. Your anger and grief make sense!

Bad churches and bad leaders are like bad parents. They

absolutely should be better. They have a sacred duty—under God—to be healthy and secure places for God's children.

The stakes are even higher for churches than for parents. The church is Christ's representative on earth. It's the place where I can meet Jesus in the flesh. No wonder Jesus had such harsh words for the faith leaders in his day. He rightly held them to the highest standard, and they had failed. They had "crushed people with unbearable religious demands and never lifted a finger to ease the burden."[1]

Thankfully, not every church is like that! No church is perfect, but some are better than others! Hopefully yours is one of the better ones. If not, go find one!

For now, I want to set aside the question of whether a church is good or bad and paint a picture of how good a church *can* be.

A COMMUNITY

A church can be a "family" where I experience safe and secure relationships. A place where I can make mistakes, break relationships and restore them. A place where God holds me close through his people. Church should also teach me information about God, but that factual knowledge needs to be lived out by the community through embodied acts of love. The embodied acts are the concrete manifestations of the truth of the facts, the "proof" that the information is true.

---

[1] Matthew 23:4 NLT

In a healthy church, I'm taught that God is lovingly interested in me, *and I can believe it* because I'm greeted by actual people who are lovingly interested in me. Loving people are God's hands and feet.

Of course, even in a healthy family there are relational ruptures. Parents yell at children; children disobey; siblings say cruel things to each other. This happens in the best of church communities too. But what matters most in childhood, as well as in church, is relational repair.

Relational rupture and repair is crucial for healthy development. It's how we learn resilience, and it strengthens our bond to those we love. When we learn that we can survive breaks and come out the other side with forgiveness and love, we become more securely attached.

This is great news for us parents! It means I don't have to be perfect (thank God!). I need to follow up after a break and seek forgiveness and reconciliation. I don't even have to do that all the time, just more often than not. It's the predictability of restored loving relationships that builds safety and trust.

I experienced this directly in a previous congregation after the church matriarch (she was the wife of a very influential member of our denomination) chewed us out for letting our kids be rowdy during service. It was very unpleasant, especially since we were trying to follow our pastor's encouragement to sit in the front row so our kids could see what was happening.

The liturgy at that church was especially well done. Our pastor had encouraged us that, "Kids behave better when they can see what's going on. No one can behave well for an hour if all you see is butts every time you stand up!" So we bravely sat on the front pew where even our shortest could see everything.

And it worked! They were more engaged with the service. We were so grateful that our kids were involved and behaving better than when they had been exiled to the extra pew by the back of the church. Of course, behaving "better" is a relative term. They still flopped on the floor, got bored and asked for tissues, gum, and the pencil from the other side of the pew. Someone still punched their brother, and someone else asked if the service was over every ten minutes. Five little kids in the front row anywhere are going to be squirrely.

Our pastor thought it was great. The noise and movement didn't faze him in the slightest. The elderly lady sitting three rows behind us on the other hand, well, she had a very different reaction. The second the service was over she marched up to the front of the church and loudly told us exactly what she thought of our parenting, and where we *should* be sitting with our family (it wasn't the front).

My wife left in tears. I was embarrassed and shocked.

Thankfully, the associate pastor saw what happened and reached out to us. He arranged for us all to meet in his office to seek reconciliation. It was terrifying, but we went. He gently helped us hear her complaint, and skillfully helped her hear our story. As soon as she heard what we were trying to do with our kids, her demeanor changed. She realized and admitted she had overreacted. She apologized and we forgave her.

We kept sitting on the front row and made a gentle effort to minimize the distractions. I don't think she ever liked that we sat there, but she never said anything about it again, and I think she moved to the other side of the sanctuary, so she didn't have to sit behind us. Our relationship was always strained, but it was also stronger than before because we shared a repair experience with her.

It wasn't a perfect reconciliation. But it was a good enough reconciliation. We all experienced God's love, kindness, and grace through each other, however imperfectly.

I wish that could happen in every relational rupture in a church. I know it can't. And many ruptures are much more serious. If repair can happen at all, it can take much longer, and may be even more imperfect. What matters is that church can be a place where we desire to make it happen. When it does, our community is stronger because we all get a concrete experience of the abstract facts we learned in Sunday school.

A church, even an imperfect one, can be a place where the community embodies God's love, delight, and grace. Through the faces of people in our church we can see delight in the face of God for us.

A COMMUNION

Church can be more than a good group of people. What defines a "community" is what they share with each other. What they commune *in*. What they *participate* in, or *partake* of, together. A community of people gather around *something* and share it with each other.

That's why food is so often associated with hospitality. We gather around the table and share food with each other. We share something in common—which is the etymology of the word "commune." A community needs something to share with each other, something to gather around.

This could be values, or a goal, or a mission. It could be work, or food, or interests. It could be all of these and more. It could be just about anything. But the distinctive thing we share in church is Jesus—his presence, love, and grace.

Church is not primarily a civic group, or a support group. It's not merely a gathering of people. It's a gathering of people around Jesus to receive the healing he wants to give to us. It's like a divinely instituted hospital. Its primary function is to forgive our sins and restore our relationship to God. And then nurse us back to health. It exists to give us direct experience of God's love, kindness, and forgiveness so that we will grow in secure attachment to him—or, in biblical terms, we will grow in faith, hope, and love towards him.

Now, before I go on, I need to do a little self-disclosure.

I'm a confessional Lutheran. That means I'm committed to the classical formulation of doctrine set forth in the *Book of Concord* that was developed by Luther and his followers.

I only bring this to your attention so you'll know where I'm coming from. I have particular doctrinal commitments about how Jesus meets us in church, and, while I'm convinced they are the correct commitments, I am not writing a defense of them. Nor am I trying to convince you of them. I'm simply sharing how I have come to experience the presence, love, and grace of Jesus in my church context. My hope is that you will be able to see through my experience to your own.

Of course, I'd be delighted if you became a confessional Lutheran too! I wouldn't be one if I didn't think it was the best option we have. But writing an apologetic for my denomination is not my goal here.

Instead, I hope to inspire you to see church as a place where Jesus is *really* present. I want to paint a picture of how church can be a place where we not only see through other people to the face of God, but where we can directly encounter God himself. Where Jesus himself is the one who does the forgiving and healing.

Perhaps you will want to explore this way of seeing church further. And hopefully that will encourage you to look for where and how Jesus is really present in your church.

SACRAMENTAL THEOLOGY

A "sacrament" in Christianity is a sign that actually does the thing signified. You are probably more familiar with this idea than you think.

For example, when the president signs a pardon for a criminal, the ceremony and the document are symbols of the criminal's pardon. At the same time, they are the actual things that do the pardoning. Or when you say "I promise…" your words are both symbols conveying your intent, and the actual act of binding yourself to a course of action. Sacraments are the same. They are signs through which God himself actually does the thing that is signified.

Here's the key thing to notice. Those that hold to a sacramental theology believe that God is concretely—not just abstractly—present and active in church. He does things physically in the here and now. We believe that Christ instituted the sacraments as specific ways that he could continue being embodied in the present fallen world. Not the *only* ways, but special ways that we can know are real because Jesus himself said they were.

For example, when a baby is baptized in my church, the water poured on their head is and signifies washing. It literally washes dirt off the body and is a sign of the spiritual washing of forgiveness which the Holy Spirit does. Yet, because of Christ's command and promises, this sign *actually and truly* accomplishes that spiritual washing—that is, forgiveness of the baby's sin. The forgiveness is as real as the water in the font. Baptism is a promise of forgiveness and adoption, of a "clean conscience" before God.[2] As a promise it is simultaneously a symbol, and the present action, of forgiveness and adoption into God's family. In other words, God himself acts in the present moment, through the sign of baptism.

Or take the reading and preaching of the Word. Whenever the Scriptures are read or correctly taught, Jesus, The Word, is speaking. The words may be coming out of the

---

[2] 1 Peter 3:21

mouth of a pastor—a mere sinful human—but they are Jesus' words. Thus they are Jesus himself.

It's important to notice that in every case it's God who is acting. From my sacramental perspective, church is not where I go to serve God. It's where I go to be served by God. It's where God is present and active and where I receive. Church is where Heaven meets earth, where God himself has guaranteed that he will forgive sins and feed his children. This means that worship is not the primary thing that happens on Sunday in church. Worship is a *response* to God loving, forgiving, and caring for us *first*.

This emphasis on God's actual presence and activity is a distinctive feature of churches with sacramental theology. We believe that God is doing very specific things—forgiveness, sanctification, and unification—through very concrete rituals and elements. I never need to wonder where Jesus is in my life. Of course, he is with me always in an intangible sense, but he is also always concrete, touchable, even audible, on Sunday morning.

Again, remember, I'm not here to convince you to believe this if you are having trouble. I'm very aware of all the questions that immediately arise if you're not familiar with this kind of thinking.

Instead, I am just asking you to see through my eyes for a moment. From where I sit, church is a very powerful—very real—secure relationship with Jesus. Every time I attend a service, God converses with me directly. He forgives my sins. He listens to my prayers. He provides for my most basic need to be known and loved and accepted unconditionally. He guarantees that he accepts me, and he unites me to himself physically.

He never requires me to do or be something *before* he does all of this. He is always moving and acting first. Church is not a reminder of the things God has done in the past, or a school room where I learn true facts about God. Church is where God is present with me, loves me, forgives me, and teaches me *right now*.

In terms of attachment, church is a weekly experience of relational repair. I spend my week doing the best I can (at least that's what I tell myself), but like every sinful child I'm inevitably disobedient. Sunday morning rolls around, and what do I hear? God himself says, "I love you, son. I forgive you. You are welcome here! I'm so delighted you are here!" And then he talks to me, sits with me, feeds me, and makes a great fuss over me like he's the best dad in all the world, and I am his favorite kid.

I know I'm loved, and I grow in trust, and I am renewed and encouraged to love others more. I mean really, how else can my heart respond when it's flooded with God's presence and love and grace?

CONCLUSION

Now, you may not agree with my sacramental commitments, but I wonder if you can find ways within your own context to shift the focus of church from being about what we do for God to what God is doing for us?

Your church, like mine, can become a powerful place to

experience the incarnate grace of God's hospitality. It can become a place where you experience a truly safe and secure relationship with God. It can become a place from which you go and do for others what Jesus has done for you.[3]

How exactly do we do that? Glad you asked! That's what the rest of the book is about.

---

[3] John 13:15

14

THE INCARNATE GRACE OF HOSPITALITY

Liv

We are vulnerable to the loving presence of God and respond in prayer; we are vulnerable to his presence in Word and Sacrament and respond in faith; we are vulnerable to the riches of his grace and respond in hospitality. Having experienced the power of welcome, the oases in the desert, we create oases for others— hospitable spaces that are grace incarnate.

WHAT IS GRACE?

Grace is real. It isn't indulgence, or leniency, or turning a blind eye to little sins and failings. It isn't even big mercy, forgiveness or gentleness. And it certainly doesn't originate in the human heart. Let's not hear again, "We just need to have a little grace for her; she didn't really mean it." Grace isn't little. Grace is big; it is real and specific.

When I was a kid in Sunday School, there was a poster on the wall with the acronym G. R. A. C. E. in bright colors. "God's Riches At Christ's Expense." A small way to teach a huge, pivotal truth. When we spoke of GRACE, we meant the dismissing of all charges against humanity because Jesus has satisfied what the Law required. We meant our status as sons and daughters of the King. Not in a cute way. Heirs and heiresses *just as much as Jesus* of eternal, physical, glorious life. We meant freedom, utter freedom. Freedom from shame. I am guiltless. Freedom from fear. I am defended. Freedom from anxiety. I have nothing to lose, nothing to risk.

Grace, won by Jesus, is innocence, dignity, freedom, security, serenity. How enormous does this word become?

My act of hospitality is God's loving presence, along with the gifts of his grace, with you in the world.

WHAT IS INCARNATE?

Literally? "En-meat-ed." I've heard a face-to-face meeting (as opposed to virtual) referred to as "in meatspace" (as opposed to cyberspace). I love that. Meatspace. I was chatting with a young woman who was having trouble with her boyfriend. They'd been dating a long time, but she was concerned that he was becoming clingy and demanding. I listened, happy to hear her process through her thoughts and feelings about the relationship, considering whether she should commit to deepening it, maybe even consider marriage.

But I began to hear a theme—every interaction between them seemed to be in words. (He said. He texted. He wrote. We talked for hours. He contacted me. I haven't heard from him.) I wondered, then suspected, then feared. So, I finally asked.

"Where does he live?"

"England."

She lives in Colorado.

"Oh, gosh, yeah. Distance can be a huge strain on a relationship. Especially a long-term one. When did you last see each other?"

She looked confused. "Well, he's trying to make a trip out here in a few months. That's why I'm so freaked out about how fast this is moving."

I persisted. "So, he used to live in Colorado, and he's been in England for a long time?"

"Oh. No. We've never been in the same place."

They'd never met.

Let me be clear. You are not in a serious relationship with a person you've never met *in meatspace*. Yes, writing, talking, video-chatting can be informative, exciting, intimate even. You might feel you have a sense of who this person is; you might feel like they're a kindred spirit, but you do not *know* a disincarnate soul. You will never know, much less honestly date, this person until you have dealings in meatspace.

Why is that? Because of our incarnate human nature. We

are both meat and immaterial; both are essential to you being you. I cannot know you if I don't know your meat-self. We do everything in, with, and under the meat that makes us up. Your soul never daydreams alone. Your brain is also daydreaming. Your feelings alone are not transported by transcendent music. Your ears, nerves, brain, spinal cord, and all your body respond to what you hear and are transported in, with, and under your feelings. We know with our whole selves—meat and soul.

I cannot have a permanent, committed marriage relationship on the spiritual plane only. There are more surface-level or functional relationships that are correspondence-only. Like my tax lady. She's super. But I'm not considering a committed relationship with her.

A marriage can never be disembodied souls drifting over the internet. It is the immaterial connection of a man and a woman through meat from the beginning. The very beginning. Like, when I first saw him sitting by the campfire wearing his mountain-man hat, and the light danced across his face. Daaaaang…. As I got to know him, spent time around him, saw how he responded to other people, the material things began to work that magic. I came to recognize the smell of his fleece jacket. If he patted my shoulder from behind to get my attention, I never thought it was someone else. I knew his touch. I came to know the actual person and, hand-in-hand with that knowing, came trust. When it came time to consider whether I wanted to marry him, well, I knew, trusted, and wanted him. It was a pretty easy decision.

If our actual marriage were immaterial, it would die. By which I mean if you want to be authentically, robustly married, you and your spouse need to have a lot of sex. And a powerful sexual relationship is material and immaterial. To have the fullest marriage relationship with your husband or wife, your souls (or whatever you want to call it) are fully present in bed through your bodies.

We live in, with, and under our bodies in all things, not only relationships. We know through our senses. Anything we've learned has come first through our senses. I can prove it to you. What is a skinned knee? You can explain it to me with terms and illustrations, but when I hear "skinned knee" I think of that moment when my blue bike (the one with the noise-making spoke beads on the wheels) skidded out on sand, and I went flying, palms and knees scraping on the pavement, pebbles embedded in the furrows. I knew it was going to hurt, so I started running home before it started to sting. Pop rushed for the peroxide, Neosporin and some of the big Band-Aids. I sniffled as he patched me up and empathized. I remember the warm pressure of his wide palm across mine through the bandage. That's a skinned knee.

What's "welcome"? Now we come to it. I can explain it, write books and poems describing it, paint pictures of what I think it looks like, but as a human, learning through my senses, incarnate, en-*meat*-ed, I can't know it until I have been present in my body to experience it. "Incarnate" means I *am* my body, and my body is me.

WHAT FEAST IS COMING?

Did you know that we will rise physically just as Jesus did? Did you know that we will live forever in a new physical world? It's amazing to me, and tragic, that a lot of Christians don't know what the eternal life that we've been promised actually is. The certain hope that we cling to is that we, en-meat-ed, will see Jesus and all believers face-to-face in a world as real as the one you're in right now.

As real as the world you're in now. Let's think about that for a second.

As a sophomore in college, I stumbled upon an amazing opportunity—to spend the Spring term at Oxford University. I'd never been to England before, but I had daydreamed about the adventure I was sure to have there. As I sat down to high tea someplace where there were tassels, Emma Thompson would walk in and ask to join me. I was pretty sure the soundtrack to *Howard's End* would play, and soon there would be at least one young gentleman in a top hat fit for Ascot and faultless cravat humbly presenting himself as a suitor. How would I let him down gently? I would return wiser, older, with a subtle wistfulness…

As it turned out, I wasn't teleported to a tea room as soon as my application was accepted. I had to buy a suitcase. I had to find my passport. I woke up in my own bed on the morning of Departure Day. I brushed my teeth. I packed Edward, my teddy bear, last. I hugged my sisters, said goodbye to Isabel, our enthusiastic seal of a sleek black mutt, who whapped me affectionately on the leg with her tail as I matched her melodic warble with my own loving nonsense. I would miss her terribly.

Then Pop and I drove into Boston, like any other day. My dad was nervous about the trip, but happy for me. He double checked the plan and gave last minute tips. A host family was meeting me when I got there. I was landing at Heathrow. "Just follow the crowd. You can ask anyone in a uniform for help. I'll come with you as far as security."

The airport smelled like an airport. Jet exhaust, car exhaust, dirty carpet, coffee, McDonalds and Cinnabon. Dropping my suitcase at check-in, fiddling with one of the many zippers in my purse, clumsily feeding my boarding pass into an inner pocket, for safety.

This was "Going to Oxford." My coffee was overfull and burned my lip. There was a cute teen couple cuddling on a bench, sharing headphones, waiting for their adventure. I was jealous. This was "Going to Oxford"?

It surprised me that a semester abroad didn't *feel* different from any other day. I didn't think it would have in it a crumpled up straw wrapper caught between the floor and the retracting wall of the gangway. I didn't account for the misty rain rolling in from Boston Harbor, making crystal beads on the bit of the plane's exterior I could see as I stepped over the gap and into the cabin.

After a week had passed, I was comfortable in a foreign land. I knew my way to Sainsbury's for groceries. I had a favorite walk: up the Thames trail, past the Perch and the ruins of Godstow Nunnery, turning West into Wytham Village, past the green and muddy fields where the early lambs were bigger every time I passed. It was crocus and daffodil when I arrived, primrose and chestnut blossoms by the time I left.

In my fantasy there had been no gravity, no smells, no changing light on the golden sandstone of Oxford. I did find a place for tea, but Emma Thompson never showed. And there was no young squire seeking me out. I lived something far, far better. What I lived was real.

From my garret room on Saint John Street (I really had a garret room with a leaded glass window I could reach from my bed, leaning over in the morning to throw the latch and let in the cool dawn air), I walked a few blocks to Gloucester Green, a cobbled square where I bought just about anything I needed at the open market. I picked up a silver-plated fish fork and knife (fancier than it sounds) which my dad later had replated and engraved as a wedding gift.

All of Oxford was open for me to explore. I had an ID card—my passport into the Oxford Student World. I was invisible on the busy streets, camouflaged in my long skirt, carrying my backpack and umbrella, like everyone else. Every eroding façade, turning side alley, and—intruding onto the sidewalk—overcrowded beds of crocus, snowdrop and daffodil gasping for air like a ballroom of corseted ladies, were mine to absorb, to sketch, to know at my own pace. I felt like a curly-headed toddler, wide eyes sweeping from gargoyle to spire, feet not always under my own control, attention suddenly caught by a beetle on a hairy vine, tight-roping between jade and waxy ivy leaves.

It goes on like this, my adventure abroad. Many more holy specificities. And my point is simple. Compare this glimpse of the real going to Oxford to my daydream of "Going to Oxford." My daydream was short, vague, and drawn from experiences I'd already had. Mostly from movies. Real Oxford—endless, involving all my senses—surprised me over and over with thoughts I'd never had, beetles I'd never seen. I could change the daydream. Oxford could change me.

What do you imagine Heaven to be like? Or maybe you know it as The New Creation? We've seen paintings of fluffy pink clouds and fat baby angels, or a Sunday School mural of the Peaceable Kingdom—serene lions and lambs, cuddled up under a sunny sky. Or maybe we've learned about the throne room of Revelation, thundering praise resonating from the throats of strange angelic creatures, saints and martyrs caught up in a celebration beyond imagining.

These bits and pieces are all we can gather, from experiences we've already had, from Scriptures we've read, and they are all metaphors. They are all a daydream of "Going to Heaven." St. John glimpsed it and could speak only from past experiences: "It was like it had been carved out of a single pearl! … It had a face like a man … six wings … horns? …" Or from Isaiah: "A kid was up to his shoulder in a snake hole but wasn't afraid. Nothing could hurt anyone!"

Daydreams. Imaginings. Not false, but certainly incomplete. And no wonder! They hadn't been there yet!

As Real Oxford was to my adorable daydream, so the

New Creation, the Great Feast, will be to all the glimpses and hints and metaphors we have from Jesus and the prophets.

Which means it will be more real than the dream. Try this. Right now. Run your thumb, flipbook style, over the edge of the pages of this book. Hear the sound? Smell the puff of paper and ink? Feel the buzz under your thumb as they flip by? See the words dance so fast you can only catch one or two? You will do this in the New Creation. Your ears will hear tiny sounds, like pages flipping. You will smell the odors of objects, just as you do now. If we rise as Jesus rose and live in a body like his, we will be able to make a little fire on a beach and cook breakfast for our friends, just as he did.

A Future, a Feast, made for incarnate beings, means that you will put food in your mouth, taste, chew, and swallow.

Maybe we've heard the expression "the wedding feast of the Lamb" referencing Heaven and thought it meant something poetic? But no! It's an actual feast, a real party! Who will play the music, I wonder? What will it sound like?

Here's how I know this is true. Remember Jesus' first miracle? The one that "showed his glory"? Jesus and his disciples were invited to a wedding, and Jesus' mother Mary was there, too. Middle Eastern wedding celebrations went on for a *week*! A week of loud music, food, drink, bright colors, dancing. The bride and groom kissed and everyone cheered. Jesus cheered!

The party was going well, and then Mary decided something was important enough to pull Jesus by the sleeve off the dance floor. What was the emergency? Were people too happy? Were they too loud? Too full of food and wine? Was it time for silence and solemn prayer? Did this joy need to be shut down? No, of course not. You know what happens next. "They have no more *wine*," she says in his ear. And who was the best person to remedy this? Mary knew. Who adds to every sweet human joy?

Jesus.

And Jesus didn't stand up and say, "I tell you the truth, blessed are those whose wine runs out. They are those who will put down their celebration and turn to prayer. Good thing this party is over. It was super loud." NO! Not my Lord! He seems to tease Mary who turns to the servers and gives the very best advice anyone ever could, "Do whatever he tells you." And what does their obedience end in? WINE. Joy. So much more time to party. This, Scripture says, he did to show his glory.

He is the God who makes a good party better.

The Feast coming is a wedding feast, and then the life we were always meant to live. I don't know what's coming exactly, but I know that if he uses a wedding to describe it, it can only be the beginning of a future full of holy specificities. His face, his voice, my life as I was always meant to live it. No more need for daydreams.

The Lord talks a lot about having betrothed us to himself. We're engaged. Under Jewish law, this means we can open a joint bank account. Everything is as official as marriage except for the last sealing act after the ceremony. It's a bold image he uses. We've drunk the first cup, pledging our commitment to be together forever once the official day comes. And now we wait. We're engaged but not together yet. Our Big Day hasn't arrived.

My own engagement lasted a year and three months! He lived in Texas, I in Massachusetts. Agony! You can bet I counted the days, tried to distract myself with work, made wedding plans and lived half out of body just longing for that day when I could get on with the life I wanted to be living: loving my man and starting our story!

Any time we visited, I breathed easier, but it wasn't quite enough. We weren't yet fully married. It was just a foretaste of the feast to come. I feel the same at communion. A minute with my Lord in a real, present way, but then it's more waiting.

This waiting puts salvation history in amazing perspective! We're still in the story! There was Creation; then we broke with him; then he patiently waited, promising to rescue us; then he bought us back and defeated our enemies, and we got engaged. But the story isn't over! He's our bridegroom, gone to prepare a place for us. He'll be back; we'll get married and get on with our real life. As sweet as a good marriage, as real as a wedding.

Our daydreams are not enough. John, the prophets, even Jesus can only give us glimpses. Something far better is coming. And our weddings, our parties, our gatherings, our tables are practice. A foretaste. Just as we meet God first in another person, we taste the New Creation with every act of hospitality.

Your welcome is not small. It is the Incarnate Grace of

Hospitality.

15

HOSPITALITY AS A POSTURE

Liv

Hospitality is more than action; it's a posture of generosity and welcome. It's who we are, living in the world in Jesus' name freely imitating his limitless love.

Hospitality is a way of being: an orientation of the heart and body toward others. It becomes a character trait more than a practice. So, what are hospitable people like? I think it's always a good idea to let C. S. Lewis explain.

Remember *The Lion, the Witch and the Wardrobe*? The four Pevensie children scramble into Narnia together for the first time. It's midwinter, bitterly cold, and they've just discovered that the only contact they have in this enchanted world, Tumnus the Faun, has been arrested for being kind to Lucy.

Their best path forward seems to be deeper into the

wood, following one little bird that flits from tree to tree, always just out of reach but not out of sight until it suddenly flies off, and the children are truly alone and suddenly hungry.

Then, an animal! Just past that tree! It beckons! Do they trust it? What choice do they have? Peter leads the way; they meet the creature, and of course it is a beaver, Mr. Beaver, and beavers are always on the right side in the stories, aren't they?

Disoriented but stepping out in faith and desperation, the children follow Mr. Beaver as the snow begins to fall again, covering their tracks. Mr. Beaver knows where he is going and presses forward until at last, the children see a frozen river, spanning the river a beaver's dam, and atop the dam, a lodge, with smoke rising from a little hole in the roof, the promise of warmth and food.

These cold, uncertain travelers enter the beaver's lodge and find domesticity. "At last!" cries Mrs. Beaver, as though they were expected. Potatoes are boiling, the kettle is on, and all pitch in to prepare and load the table with a satisfying meal.

What is it about the Beavers that makes the children trust them? It is their hospitality—a natural posture of generosity and welcome, sharing what they have and who they are. What provision of food and shelter the Beavers have is simple enough, but that doesn't make the marmalade roll that appears at the end of the meal any less miraculous. This warmth and acceptance echoes something much bigger and more powerful—abundant and ever-surprising love.

Love is the power behind this marmalade roll. On its own, it might be tasty, but as the end of a desperately needed meal, and the beginning of the most significant conversation the children have ever had, it *is* love and trust, as vulnerable and funny as their appetites for dessert and their sticky fingers and lips as they eat it together.

When all are filled and happy, they lean back in their chairs, sigh and talk. Now we finally hear the heart of the matter. Mr. and Mrs. Beaver live the way they do, industrious, fruitful, in good spirits, because they have hope—strong and certain hope that they are being delivered from the tyranny of the White Witch and her eternal winter. Spring is coming; Aslan is on the move.

Who would hunker in his cold hovel, hoarding his resources and avoiding his neighbors, if freedom, hope, joy, warmth and victory were sweeping down on him? This meal is so much more than food. They will meet Aslan and celebrate in the open! This is a foretaste of the feast to come! Marmalade roll and all!

The Beavers' hospitality comes as second nature because it is in the name of Aslan. They are not following some social rule, manipulating impressionable guests, or bragging. They are living in the posture of generosity and welcome common to folk who have hope and eager expectation of joy.

SHARE WHAT YOU HAVE—YOU ARE ENOUGH

My hope, like Mr. and Mrs. Beaver's, is certain. Because I

am a forgiven and beloved child of God, living in eager expectation of my permanent home, I have nothing to lose by loving the people around me. I can share what I have and who I am, right now, with those put in my path. Which means I am enough. I am acceptable. I am provided for. I am where I should be, and I have what I need, and more. I have acceptance to share, provision to share, a sense of purpose and significance to share.

Generosity is the fruit of freedom. If I've been holding my breath and my belongings in anxiety, generosity is a release of this tension, an exhalation in the confidence that Jesus has got me covered. He knows the things I need; he is serious when he says I can trust him to care for ALL my needs. I can let go. I can breathe out. I can open my hand for the good of those around me. Unconstrained by the belief that my effort or skill will be my savior, I can live in freedom, knowing that I can do my work fully aware that Jesus doesn't need my effort and my anxious grasp on resources to provide for me, my children, or my friends.

If Jesus works through you to love the world, and he does, then whatever you are and have is enough. We are all different, with different resources, contexts, abilities, personalities. I am free to share what I have, but I am not called to share what I don't have.

I share what I have, not what I wish to have, or what I feel I ought to have. I've been a guest at some super fancy houses. Exhausted one summer, I visited a friend who lives by the sea. Smiling, she hugged me, settled me into a wicker chaise longue on her wrap-around porch, put a chilled white wine in my hand, and treated me like royalty. I felt accepted and cared for in these luxurious surroundings.

I've also been a guest at Auntie Joanne's tiny apartment over the funeral home in downtown Westminster. It was our traditional New Year's Day indoor picnic, and she gave me and my sisters giant candy canes! I remember feeling so welcome, so important, *so fancy*!

The guest crossing my threshold needs welcome and acceptance more than anything in the world. I have that to offer!! Whether I set a table on my pool deck for brunch or spread a tablecloth on the clear area of carpet in my apartment, my powerful, life-enriching gift is the welcome and acceptance I have to give.

Share what you have, not what you wish you had. Don't apologize; don't wait until you have something "better" to offer. You have what others need. You are enough. Welcome and acceptance will make your guests feel like a million bucks, even if it only costs you five.

SHARE WHO YOU ARE—YOUR WELCOME IS ENOUGH

Your welcome is far more than *your* welcome. We live in Jesus' name. Out of our freedom, we are free to extend whatever abundance the Lord has poured into our hands at this moment. At Signpost Inn, we say that the first place we meet God is in another person. God is present in a believer's gesture of acceptance, forgiveness, provision, peace, joy, patience. Love. Your welcome, on its own, is Jesus' incarnate grace.

Your welcome, *as it is*, is enough. I hope you don't hear me calling you to make your welcome as big as the love of God. I hope you hear that the big love of God becomes as small as we are, for us.

We are incarnate. God, in Jesus, is incarnate. He stretched the sky over the world and became an embryo in Mary's uterus.

When Mary, newly pregnant with God the Embryo, visited her cousin Elizabeth, John the six-month-embryo convulsed with joy and Elizabeth knew instantly that the mother of her Lord had come to visit. Elizabeth's greeting, her welcome, was enough! What more could she offer than faith coming out to meet Mary and our incarnate God with joy? Mary met with acceptance and love in Elizabeth's open arms, which God was showing her also by choosing her to bring us God-enmeated.

Elizabeth literally met God in another person. Her welcome of Mary, in the name of God, welcomed God in Mary, and Mary's arrival brought God to Elizabeth! It's a head-spinning whirlwind of the love of God! A little bit like the Trinity.

The posture of hospitality, opening a door and greeting a guest for Jesus' sake, is a proclamation of the gospel. I am speaking grace to this dear human out of the hope I have in my secure future. The welcome I offer is far more than the welcome *I* offer. My small gesture, sharing who I am and what I have, is the Lord working his loving presence in the world. It is the incarnate grace of hospitality.

16

HOW TO HOSPITALITY

Liv

How do we make this beautiful ideal happen in the real world? Hospitality, a habit of sharing what I have and who I am with others, plays out in the details—those holy specificities. I can tell you, "Be hospitable!" But it's terrifying to leap without help.

USE THIS FRAMEWORK

1. A guest
2. A space
3. A time frame
4. A consumable
5. A loosely-committed-to activity

LET'S UNPACK THAT

1. A guest

Start with people you know really well. Maybe think of two people who get along. What do they like?

For the sake of the exercise, you've chosen Nikki and Mel. They're the middle-aged married couple who took you under their wing when you moved to town. She teaches high school art.

2. A space

Considering their abilities and what is convenient for you and them, think of a space you can open for these guests.

They've had you over lots of times, but you've never felt like your apartment is "enough" to have guests in. Let's change that. You clear off your table and decide to host them at your place. Good for you! That's very brave!

3. A time frame

The only minute you have between now and November is this Saturday morning, from 9 to 11. You usually sleep in on Saturday, but this matters. You can book the time.

4. A consumable

Here's where you can help your guest feel at ease. This time frame doesn't cover a traditional meal hour, which is great! Serve snacks and ask them to bring one snack they really love. If that means the menu is honey mustard pretzels and a bowl of grapes, that's great! Oh, and maybe that fun lemonade you've been meaning to try!

(Note: This is literally any consumable. It might be cookies, but it might be a cigar, or art supplies. Just something to put your hand to and use up. Pro level: It can even be doing dishes or folding laundry. But that's next-level stuff.)

5. A loosely-committed-to activity

Here's the secret: The activity is a cover. The point of this time is to create a space of generosity and welcome with these precious humans—incarnate grace. What you actually plan on can change! Let's say you decide to ask Nikki to bring over a simple art project she does with her students and teach you guys. It is generous of you to defer to her, and it's fun for her to teach Mel who never gets to see her in the classroom.

But if you finish the project really quickly, or Nikki forgets an important element at home, you can change gears. Nothing is ruined. Ask her about her favorite projects she's ever done or about memorable students. You've set up a welcoming space where she and Mel can tell you about their lives while you enjoy your snacks.

The time, seen this way, is never a failure. Getting humans to spend generous and welcoming time with other humans is a win.

PRACTICE: A FEW MORE SCENARIOS

Here are a few more scenarios to help you think through

this framework. Observe, copy, and improvise. Are there similar scenarios in your life? How might you use this framework to provide hospitality?

Scenario One:

1. The guest: Jess who is very quiet and doesn't really do eye contact
2. The space: One end of the ½ mile riverwalk to the other
3. The time frame: One hour before you have to go to work
4. The consumable: A drink from the coffee shop you both parked near
5. The loosely-committed-to activity: A stroll the length of the riverwalk, BUT you see a cool boulder and sit there instead, just watching the river and being present

Scenario Two:

1. Your cousin, Abby, who just had a baby
2. Her bedroom where she's recovering from birth
3. 30 minutes before she needs to take a nap
4. Fresh peaches sliced up on a pretty plate
5. Hearing her birth story BUT she ends up suddenly emotional and needs to cry while you hold the baby

Scenario Three:

1. Josh, Adam, and Joe who need other men they can be real with
2. Your garage, with a few chairs pulled up around a utility bin as a coffee table
3. 6-8 pm because one gets up early and can't stay super late
4. Cigars, obviously. Probably some whiskey
5. Each guy gets a chance to say whatever he needs to. No interruptions, no advice, only questions

Scenario Four:

1. Theresa and Sam, a couple you knew from way before they were married who are in town and want to see you
2. Your kitchen table and living room
3. 6 pm until the conversation is over; you're willing and able to let this one go long
4. Family dinner—whatever suits everyone, maybe they bring a dessert?
5. Catching up, talking theology, following the conversational rabbit trail, BUT they brought a really funny game, so you play a while and laugh your heads off

LET'S PRACTICE THE PROCESS:

Your turn. Here's the framework; experiment with it! Feel free to write your ideas in the space below or use your own journal.

1. A guest

2. A space

3. A time frame

4. A consumable

5. A loosely-committed-to activity

You've made a tentative plan! That's great! It gets easier the more you do it.

17
HOW TO HOSPITALITY: A GUEST

Liv

If we're going to live hospitably, we'll have to be where humans are, and even invite them into a space with us. It's going to be intimate, real, and awkward. I'm terrified of being awkward, so I have avoided extending hospitality or partaking in it. But I want to assure you, awkwardness is ok!

Embrace awkwardness: it's ok! I don't know about you, but I have a tiny pang of panic when I know I'm about to be around people. Even if I know and love them and have spent tons of time with them, I get a crawly feeling and a moment of foggy disorientation just before human engagement. Somehow I imagined that the feeling of being a "freshman" would have dissipated by now. Surely the more I attended events and had conversations, the easier it should get? Well, sometimes and kind of, but really I have not left the awkward freshman behind. She is right there, ready to make it weird.

Do you feel the same around people? Guess what? You're not weird; that's normal.

Human beings in a room with other human beings are awkward. You'd think we'd have figured out, as a species, how to speed past the painful bit and slide into acquaintance and friendship gracefully. But that's not possible. Humans are awkward.

It's not just you. And I find that helpful.

Ours is a lonely generation, desperate to be found and included. We're all afraid that no one will come after us, no one is interested in us, no one wants to hear our stories. You feel that way. Other people feel that way. One guest at a time, we need to be the hero who creates a pocket of welcome in the world and reaches out a hand to one person at a time.

There's just no comfortable way to do this. Others feel just like you do: conflicted. They want to be asked over, and the last thing they want is to be asked over. They want to go out, and they want to stay home. They want to be heard and ignored. It's ok. We *need* connection but are scared of it. And in the end, connection is far more satisfying than hiding under a blanket re-binging that show. Hospitality is life-giving, and it's worth the awkwardness, I promise.

LET THE LITTLE CHILDREN COME TO ME

What's worth the awkwardness? You are. If I ask you out

to coffee, and I sit across the table from you, feeling all crawly and nervous, I remember that the most important person is the one sitting across from me. You.

I feel small and unimportant most of the time, and I know you do too. But Jesus is here for us unimportant ones. When you feel like you're less: less deserving, less interesting, less experienced, you are right in that crowd of little children that Jesus welcomed. "Let the little children come to me," he said, scolding his disciples. "I am here for the least of these. When you welcome one of them, you welcome me."

You are worth my time. And in this time, the welcome that exists at that table is enough. In fact, it's enormous. If you and I are both "the least of these," a moment of kindness like this between us is everything Jesus called us to. Love one another; welcome one another. Whatever we've done for the least of these, we've done for Jesus.

We can choose, in a posture of hospitality, to see Jesus in everyone who needs a minute of acceptance. Everyone who needs anything from us! Everyone who needs to be a guest. And I'm not speaking metaphorically! We participate in the huge love of God toward humanity when we serve anyone for the sake of Jesus.

HOW? PRACTICAL ADVICE

Start small. Do you work at a coffee shop? Serve your guest her latte and imagine Jesus' hand receiving it. Do you care for kids? Answer their endless questions as though Jesus were the one asking. I know it's hard to imagine Jesus having any needs, or allowing us to fill them! It seems disrespectful to give Jesus something, to help him. But he told us that whatever we do for least of these (anyone!), we have done for him. So, see him when you offer what you have and who you are to another person.

That is the incarnate grace of hospitality. Big realities flowing through our small hands. Serving a latte or answering a question is a small action, and that is as it should be. We don't make ourselves big enough for God; he has made himself small enough for us. I don't need to serve *miraculous* lattes; Jesus is present for my pretty good latte, handed over with a normal level of human love.

So sitting across the table from you, feeling human awkwardness but welcoming you anyway, I am extending the incarnate grace of hospitality to you—the welcome guest.

Take a minute to think about how great it feels to be that guest, and how little anyone really has to do to make you feel that way. When someone expresses interest in spending time with me, listening, being present for a minute, it is a high point in my month. I'll probably remember it all year, to be honest. You have the power to welcome "one of the least of these," one of God's kids, as your guest—a simple act.

So whom will you invite?

INCONVENIENT FRIENDSHIPS

Since we were talking about awkwardness, let's dive right in. The world needs welcome. Who is the world? For each of us, the world first means the people we bump elbows with frequently. We may not have much in common or even really like each other, but we are in each other's world—up close and present—but not.

We keep distance from uncomfortable social connections, especially the daily ones, so though we may be up close with each other, we are not often present. Brandon and I call these "inconvenient friendships."

We are in community with, let's say, fellow middle school teachers at work. We attend compulsory training sessions together, but we don't bother to reach out past the coworker to the person. It would be inconvenient and awkward to assume they need anything; I may be lonely, but surely no one else is?

I think you know where I'm heading. If I feel it, others do too. If I've asked, "Why doesn't anyone care??," you can bet your coworkers have. That teacher, Marcy, might go home to an empty house and replay her day over and over in her head, unable to shake the feeling that everyone hates her. Why not sit down on the bench between sessions, reintroduce yourself and say something like, "So glad it's still warm enough to sit outside!"

This is a gesture that shows that you know she exists and is worth talking to. As small as it seems, this is hospitality that creates connection—welcoming someone into who you are and what you have right now. We all need human connection, and who is going to take the risk if you don't?

The term, "inconvenient friendship" is a little tongue-in-cheek, of course. Calling someone "inconvenient" is pretty merciless. The phrase just helps me notice my unwillingness to put myself out there, even for a walk or short outing, with someone who (I have lied to myself) is perfectly content in their own life and doesn't need to feel welcomed. Not everyone wants to chat all the time, but everyone wants to feel acknowledged and valued. So consider who your "inconvenient friends" are!

Truly! Take a minute here and think through your contexts: work, school, church, home, clubs, sports. Live in a small town? It could be the guy you always nod at while you're walking your dog, or the old lady across the street who occasionally pays your son for yard work. Got someone in mind?

It's going to be awkward much of the time. It's how we are. So we're off the hook! We can't change it, and it's not just you. So go to the church potluck! Stand around during coffee hour with the people whose faces you've seen but names you don't know! It's simple: presence, eye contact, telling and hearing each other's stories (interesting and otherwise). It is what life is made of. It's how we are loved, and how we love. Someone asks your name (again) and listens to your story with curiosity. You ask them theirs (again), and they make you laugh. You'll be surprised how quickly people open up and how quickly you'll feel more comfortable.

I think many of my most important relationships began out of inconvenient friendships. Awkward park dates, small talk at a dinner function, even square dancing at a school fundraiser! It's never been easy to be at ease. No period of history has been any better at it. So dive in. Spend time with the humans that are near you. It's so important—for them and for you.

PRACTICE STARTING SIMPLE

Ok, after the terrifying prospect of a hospitality cold call to an inconvenient friend, this practice should feel easy! Do you have a significant other, or a son, daughter, sibling or close friend that you feel at ease with? Literally ask if they'll practice being your guest!

Remember our framework: pick a guest, a space, a time frame, a consumable, and a loosely-committed-to activity, and give it a shot! For example:

> "Hi, Mom!" (a guest)
>
> "I'm practicing hospitality! Could we meet at the Duck Park?" (a space)
>
> "For an hour on Saturday, starting at 11?" (a time frame)
>
> "I'll bring some duck food!" (a consumable – for the ducks!)
>
> "We can feed the ducks!" (a loosely-committed-to activity)

Now, give yourself a break (and a treat!). It feels awkward to ask. Remember, the asking and the beginning of a visit do feel awkward, but within a few minutes it'll sort itself out.

Repetition makes it easier, and it makes you better at it. After you've practiced by inviting someone you know really well, ask yourself who you might invite into your hospitable space next! Each time you enrich a guest's life, you enrich your own as well. You'll collect the physical means to do it more spontaneously and efficiently. You might buy a basket for a quick picnic with your sister one day, and then you have a basket ready to go when you invite someone else who intimidates you a little…but you're armed with this cool little basket!

18
HOW TO HOSPITALITY: A SPACE

Liv

As you practice inviting people to share what you have and who you are, within our manageable framework, it will become easier. Your comfort and your instincts will change and so will your surroundings, bit by bit, into a space formed by and for hospitality. Like the picnic basket picked up for one invitation and now available for many more, you'll notice that you become equipped for welcome.

You may not be ready to host a banquet, but are you able to offer a mug of tea to a friend? Set it up: call your guest, set the space, the time frame, the consumable (tea of course!), and a loosely-committed-to activity. And then, before your friend comes over, you might realize you only have one mug that you really like. You don't feel like offering tea in a mug with a gas station logo on it (how did you even end up with that mug?). A quick run to Goodwill, and voila! Seventy-five cents later, you are set forever to offer a friend tea in a mug you like! Your life is being transformed by generosity and welcome.

Little changes in your surroundings will make it easier to offer welcome. And I have found these changes only happen when a guest is imminent. It's an exercise in futility to wait until your space is "ready to receive a guest." You will never feel ready. But the point is not for you to feel ready; it is to offer incarnate grace to another human desperately in need of welcome.

A friend of mine is reclaiming her own space after a personal tragedy. Her goal in cleaning, repairing, and replacing the broken bits of her past is hospitality! She knows how life-giving generosity and welcome are. She has received it, and she wants to give it! Her space, her life, and a little bit her heart, can be renewed by giving hospitality. She is not waiting until her yard is "good enough." She wants to refresh her yard as an offering of incarnate grace to us, her friends.

My own home has been formed this way, too. Our old front door, solid with no glass, used to open into a small, dark entryway. We greeted guests uncomfortably close-up and with at least one shoulder touching a wall. This was not sustainable for a home which is open for ministry and large gatherings every week. An amazing donor funded a remodel that opened it all up, and now it is comfortable and full of natural light, with a line of sight back to the kitchen, where we gather.

Offering welcome creates a space equipped for welcome. A heart similarly disposed becomes similarly equipped.

ONE SPACE IS ENOUGH

Many of my fondest memories as a welcomed guest take place in one room, or even in one part of one room. Any semi-cleared spot can be a space for acceptance: a place to be received. I don't have to go crazy getting my entire house "company-ready" for my visiting friends to be loved. The point is welcome, which is achievable—not perfection, which is not.

When I was in college, some of my friends hosted "Tuesday Toast Nights" in their dorm room. It was literally toast. On Tuesdays. In a dorm room. For a bunch of awkward, unconnected freshmen, nothing was more encouraging than someone inviting us over for a piece of toast and jam. It was so ridiculously simple, so very homey.

These guys were all smiles, goofy jokes and warm inclusion. Everyone who filtered in and out of that little room, balancing buttered toast on their fingers, left with the glow of friendship. And no one ever noticed that their closet was crammed full of dirty laundry and Hot Pocket wrappers. The guys supplied the space we needed; they didn't try to put their whole room, closets and drawers, in order first. They didn't need to be perfect. And neither do I. The welcome is enough.

TRAVEL LIGHT!

Offering welcome is going to come with a cost. Whether it's a few dollars for tea and biscotti (that actually sounds really good right now—I know what my next writing break treat will be!), or a few hundred for a big party, the real cost will likely be emotional. The greatest cost is usually having to give up our need for control.

You're stepping out in faith, trusting that the world needs welcome, and that your modest efforts can fill that need. But the old voice in the back of your head says things like "What if the bathroom isn't clean *enough*?," "What if they're judging me for ____?," and hardest of all sometimes, "What if they move or break something?"

Welcoming others in, whether it's inconvenient friendships or old pals, requires another step of faith: that you are being provided for by your Heavenly Father. Your physical surroundings, like everything else God entrusts you with, do not finally belong to you. You are a caretaker, not an owner. Things will be lost and broken. Let me share what might be a new vocabulary word with you. I first read it on sign somewhere and had to look it up:

CAUTION: FRANGIBLE!

I love that word. It just means "breakable," but it's way more fun to say. With five kids, a husband, and frequent guests in the house, things do break. Most often it's something unimportant, but once in a while it's something precious. The smash of glass, the crack of a breaking chair, can cause a similarly destructive emotional response, but it doesn't have to. I can be ready for this inevitability.

When something breaks, I say aloud "Travel light!" I'm a pilgrim and a wanderer in this world. I share what I may have with fellow travelers, and I have so much! I don't expect to keep and carry all my stuff all through my journey. A heavy backpack would slow me down. Travel light! Let things go when they break. Phew! What a relief!

Objects, ordinary and precious, are frangible. But they were always going to be temporary; you don't take it with you, right? I use my space and welcome others into it, even if there's collateral damage to objects. The smash of a glass or crack of a chair leg is a call: "Travel light!"

It's an act of will, at least at first, to acknowledge that ownership belongs to God. God has given me things to steward. But they belong first to Him, so I follow promptings to use them the way he wants. Extending welcome to an en-meated soul in the name of Jesus is *so* much more valuable than that robin's-egg-blue plate I bought on that beautiful summer trip. I make the choice to love the human more than the plate. Funny when you think of it that way.

You have no obligation to the objects. You don't belong to objects; they belong to you. You are free to use (up!) the objects in your care.

Letting go of the illusion of control *frees* me for welcome, for love. I am provided for; my cup overflows; I don't need to grasp onto anything. Open those hands.

JAMMIES OR TUXES: THE PUZZLE OF AUTHENTICITY

We open our hands, abandoning to the Lord our perceived needs, recalling his kindness and provision over the years, choosing to believe that he will provide our daily bread. This is a choice, a skill, a habit, even a spiritual discipline. But it's an ironic one. I work and work and choose and struggle… to release. It's an act of faith to accept provision, acceptance, love.

I am provided for. I am loved. I *can* share what I have and who I am with those around me. The welcome itself is enough. It's everything. What is incarnate grace other than a physical expression of unconditional welcome?

I don't have to defend my space or wait until it's "good enough." I am enough. My space is enough. The welcome is enough. My space is ready to receive the most important person (the one across from me right now) and to offer a powerful welcome, God's welcome. Hear me—my space is ready right now.

It takes some serious vulnerability to let someone into my "not good enough" space. The more unhappy I am with the place, the harder it is to believe that I could be worthy to give incarnate grace. I forget so quickly that I am totally accepted by God and can be myself offering hospitality. And there are many ways for people to be! Many ways to host! My real welcome might look very different from your real welcome. No matter what I have to offer, it's all offered in love for you. No pressure, no judgement. Messy or tidy, I can offer incarnate grace.

If you're the kind of person whose home (like mine) tends to be "in process," I encourage you to what I've heard called "scruffy hospitality." Scruffy hospitality says to your friend with all those kids, "Come over after Emmie's dance practice! I'll make spaghetti!" You're not "ready" for formal entertaining. Floor unswept, clean laundry in a pile on the couch. But your friend might cry when you offer a quick spaghetti stop to her and her scrappy crew. (Is Ethan even wearing shoes?) You know why she'll cry? Because you accept her, and her kids!, as a person needing love who doesn't want to wait for help until the helper is tidy enough and has matching silverware. She needs love. Now. In the shape of a bowl of spaghetti and someone else cleaning up after.

I know that a tableful of little kids is some people's Everest. You don't need to start there. Scruffy hospitality might mean being aware at 8 pm (after you've put your jammies on) that you have a couple free hours this evening and a half-bottle of wine. Call that friend over for a glass and an hour chat? If it's a close friend, I dare you not to change out of your pj's! You are declaring loudly that you believe that your welcome is enough, even in your end-of-day get-up. (Glasses and scrunchy?)

On the other hand, I might be a person who loves my tidy, well-stocked home and is eager to share my cute mugs and teas with people. My "real and authentic" self gets so much joy out of my matching tea set and biscuit tin ready at all times with chocolate-dipped orange shortbread (...next writing break!).

My guest is important enough to offer my real self, but scrupulously bringing my real self is not the point. The point is giving my guest something I hope they'll like because I do, but holding their approval with an open hand, because what matters is the power of the welcome itself.

I bring my real self, offering what I really am and have, but I also keep in mind, in general, the needs of this specific, beloved guest. I have a very dear friend who suffers from true OCD, a handicap which has made their life very difficult. They are fighting and seeking healing (hooray!), but it would be terribly unwelcoming of me to insist that I show "scruffy hospitality" in order for me to be "real." When they visit, I clean the bathroom with special care. I make sure there's not an obvious stumbling block to their being able to accept love and welcome in my space (like a dog poop on the porch). Now, I cannot anticipate everyone's needs, and I certainly can't force anyone to have happy feelings! But I can consider whether this is a moment for full jammy time or a bit more careful preparation.

Both approaches are real. Both are loving. Most of all, both approaches are for the sake of the guest! Incarnate grace for my friend suffering from OCD is expressed in gentleness. I'm not going to throw them into exposure therapy for the sake of my humble brag about my messy house.

If I am self-righteous in my "scruffy hospitality," I am not sharing who I am and what I have with those around me. I'm posturing. And that's ugly. The beautiful approach is to assess what this guest might need (in broad terms), and support that. Remember that it is the welcome that is enough. Offer welcome as though you are enough, because you are. And your space is enough, messy or tidy, because it is.

What about fancy tea parties??? I'm glad you asked. You in glasses and scrunchy is the real you. So is the you all gussied up for the big event. Hospitality funnels God's present love to the person across from you. Are you willing to be that conduit, messy or tidy? Then lovely. You are totally free to have a super duper frilly, fancy tea party as your authentic self and offer incarnate grace to your guests.

Are you the dude in this equation? Did your lady really just ask you to help throw a tea party?? What if you're really not feeling it?? That's ok! You don't have to have all the right feelings for the event to express love. Remember, it is not your feelings that have the power. It is your welcome. Trust love. Wear a tux. (Brandon here: and remember dude, you look good in a tux!)

But ok, there's a middle ground. A guest is coming to a simple dinner, and you don't want a "jammies" kind of visit. You bark (just a little) at the kids to help get things straightened up. Quick-clean the bathroom. Dining room table cleared off and wiped down. Real plates! Maybe a candle? This isn't fake, and it's not overkill. It's lovely to work hard for a minute to make it nice. You don't have to! But you may! And hand over to the Lord your fears of having the wrong motivations. "Maybe this is posturing?" No one's heart is perfectly in line at all times. Just remember that the point of this dinner is a moment of connection and acceptance between dear humans. That is enough.

AWAY FROM HOME

Happily, there are spaces I don't have to prepare. Hospitality is not limited to my home. Consider the template above. A guest, a time frame, a consumable, and a loosely-committed-to activity: incarnate grace can come together anywhere!

A couple of the examples I gave above took place at the park or at another person's house. Everything about hospitality serves to create a space of physical welcome to another dear en-meated soul. Find little ways to make it special to your guest and choose any space you like!

If the outing is at the park, throw a blanket in your car in case you decide to sit on the grass. If it's a walk on a trail or in these parts a hike up a fourteener (if you don't know that that means, you're not from Colorado; don't feel bad), make sure you know where you're going and that it's practical for this visit. Keep outings very simple 99% of the time. Remember, it's not about the outing. It's all an excuse to be a loving, physical presence with the dear humans because Jesus is, and it's all about him loving us after all.

The space can be a café, restaurant, or heck, a mini golf course! Just keep in mind that the welcome is for the other person, never for you to show off or intimidate. When extending welcome away from home, choose a place that works for your guest—the most important person.

19

HOW TO HOSPITALITY: A TIME FRAME

Liv

A time frame is fundamental to creating a realistic space of welcome.

We only have so much time. As finite humans, sharing who we are and what we have cannot be without limit, and of course that includes our time.

My constant fear is that "it's not enough," or to be honest, that "I'm not enough." To address this fear, I imagine that if I'm going to love and welcome someone "well enough," surely I need to offer limitless access to my time and resources! Well, how does that feel? Daunting. Impossible. In my head I start to think it's mean of the other person to need so much! Before I even make a plan, I'm already resenting my guest! It's understandable, but it's just my fear of not being enough.

I feel these things too, and it's been helpful to embrace my little-ness: Jesus loves little me; my space is a little space, and my time comes in seconds, minutes and hours, not eternities (not on this side of Heaven, anyway).

The pressure is off! Humans live in time, and it's ok to love them in moment-sized spaces. At Signpost Inn, we say that "The most important time is the present. The most important person is the one you're with. The most important work is love." None of these guidelines say, "To be enough, you need to give up your personal life to open-ended spaces of welcome forever." Not at all. Your guest is a finite human, and so are you. Setting a time frame makes a little space for finite beings to taste a digestible bit of the infinite love of our welcoming God.

Remembering that the welcome is enough, I can suit the time frame to the space I want to create. I'll give two examples here: Signpost Inn Evening and Easter Feast. Both examples here are more hefty than a park visit, so keep in mind that even the shortest moment has the same welcoming power as either of these examples. But even these examples are designed with a time frame in mind.

SIGNPOST INN EVENING:

Living within time and setting a time frame, I feel free to keep a welcoming space simple and repeatable. Our home is open on Wednesday nights for Signpost Inn Evenings. We tell people they can drop in any time between 7-10ish pm. My family expects this every Wednesday, so they know that this time is set apart for this purpose. It's not "our home is open unpredictably forever." No matter how idyllic that sounds, it's not practical for us, and I suspect that those who really try to create a truly "revolving door" home face burnout and resentment eventually. Your home can be privately yours sometimes.

And that goes for the end of the evening. If I've gotten into an intense conversation, or if someone needs a minute at 10:05, I have the freedom to extend a bit more time to this guest, or the freedom to appeal to the hour and it being "time for bed." On the right evening, with certain understanding friends, we might even say, "Ok! It's 10:30! Everyone out! See you next time!"

An expressed time frame is a kindness. It helps everyone know that it's ok for them to be there. Within this time frame we may all rest and reconnect, and we have the freedom to be completely present, in this sacred moment of welcome: 7–10ish pm on Wednesdays.

EASTER FEAST

There are times for a big, loud, inconvenient, disruptive welcome within a crazy time frame, too! You'll read more about this event later, so I won't go into detail here, but on the night before Easter Sunday, we prepare for a midnight Easter Feast to celebrate the resurrection of our Lord at the first possible moment! We tell our guests to arrive at 11:50 pm for a brief time of silence and reflection by a bonfire in the front yard where Brandon leads in a few readings. Then the doors are flung wide at midnight with a cry of "Christ is Risen!!!" The candles inside are all lit, the music blares, and we feast and toast our Risen King!

The time frame here is 11:50 pm until whenever. Intentionally, there is no cut-off time to this welcome. We have had years of merry feasting only until 2 am, and we have had years of an after-party around the bonfire outside starting at 3 am and lingering on until a couple guests have tumbled onto couches or into the guest room. Those are years of very bleary-eyed church attendance only a few hours later! Worth it, though.

How can I say that Easter Feast is planned within a time frame if people may leave within one hour or in the morning? Well, here is a huge secret. I have preparations of ALL kinds, ALL day on Holy Saturday, and although I love my friends and community, almost no one other than my children has ever been invited to come before 11:50 pm. In those daytime hours of preparation, cleaning, baking, and cooking, I am pondering the suffering, crucifixion, death, and burial of Our Lord, and the confusion and sorrow of the disciples as they grieved the end of all their hopes. It is a core time in the church year, which marks the passage of time by living through the events of Jesus' life from Advent through Ascension. Holy Week, leading up to Easter, is the slow time, and I want it all to myself and my family. I do not really budge on this time frame because this time is spoken for.

And then! When midnight comes, we can all be free to give and share this time without reservation or regret!

THE HOLY HOUR: THE HUMAN ATTENTION SPAN

Purely practical advice: You have probably experienced this yourself, but maybe you haven't noticed how often it happens. I don't know why, but the best conversations come to a natural pause at the 60-minute mark. It is also true that a difficult meeting or an awkward reunion struggles and flops about for a bit, finds a rhythm, and settles down at about 60 minutes as well. Creating a space of welcome within a one-hour time frame is almost always your best bet. Thirty minutes is usually too short, an hour and a half is often too long. An hour—one set-apart, holy, human hour is realistic and repeatable.

20

HOW TO HOSPITALITY: A CONSUMABLE

Liv

In a nightmare about hosting, I sit in a stiff-backed chair across a slightly-too-small table from a person who looks me directly in the eye. What do we talk about? Why are we here?? Why am I not wearing pants??? (Told you it was a nightmare.)

Happily, reality is not quite as scary as that, but we all have trepidation in company, feeling we don't know what to do or say. There's hope! Once we have our guest, our setting, and our time frame, we can turn to the fourth element of welcome for the dear humans: a consumable!

Providing a consumable creates an automatically shared experience. Food and drink are the most obvious. We meet at a pub for a beer and fried stuff. (Poll: pickles, mushroom caps, or mozzarella sticks?) Let's say your guest chooses the spot. Great! They feel comfortable in familiar surroundings. Let's say you choose. Great! You are sharing something you like, which is a very real vulnerability move. Beer and fried stuff make it easier for awkward humans to be near each other. We all eat! We can all talk about what we eat! And remember: this is all just an excuse to share who you are and what you have with another glorious immortal being… who just really loves ranch with mozzarella sticks!

Beer not your speed? How about The London Tea Room in downtown St. Louis? Commenting on the rich, floral, herby perfume of all the teas as you walk in, picking a table, looking around and settling in, our inner mammal alert and gauging and becoming convinced we are safe (it's what we do!). All these behaviors ready us for connection, and when the Earl Grey and fresh scones with Devonshire cream arrive, well! We share our en-meated ability to raise simple wheat and leaves to the attention of immortal beings, bringing significance to the consumables and a moment of connection between people. Powerful stuff!

(Also: visit St. Louis so you can stop by The London Tea Room. We miss it terribly. If you feel moved to send the author a thank you gift, order me some loose-leaf).

Still sound pretty involved? Too fancy? Here's the miracle of a food consumable: it can be the simplest thing in the world, offered as a sign of welcome and connection. Really. It seems too easy, but it is the medium that connects people, something all our hands reach for. The bag of chips you thought to pick up, or the bowl of peanuts you took the time to put on the counter when the guys arrive, *is* the welcome, in physical form. Memories of welcomes offered to me with a consumable have formed me and stayed with me for decades. It wasn't the food; it was the welcome. En-meated. Or sometimes en-fruited. For example:

A BOWL OF CHERRIES

Fourteen is a tough age. I remember the feeling. I didn't quite deserve a spot at the adults' table, but I wanted to be respected and included. I expended a lot of effort trying to be acceptable, but I felt I just hadn't earned it yet.

And then a picnic. I don't even remember the occasion. But I recall, like a photograph, a bowl of fresh cherries, set on a blanket in the grass by the Clinton Dam in Massachusetts. It was a beautiful spot to gather a few people on a sunny afternoon. And that ceramic bowl of cherries had been put there *for me*. And by whom? By one of the most admirable adults in my life: the headmistress of my school! *For me!*

I was included! I was accepted! I hadn't done anything to earn my spot at this picnic blanket, on this sweep of grassy hill! It was just grace; it was just richness and welcome. I, an awkward and often unpleasant fourteen-year-old, was welcome in this group of people I admired. I belonged among them.

As a guest, I received the incarnate grace of hospitality: acceptance in the bodily form of a bowl of cherries on a blanket. Acceptance tastes like cherries!

I promise you, it is the welcome—expressed in the language of food and drink—that is enough. And you can be prepared to offer a handy consumable—just something to create a shared experience and put your guest at ease—in your own home, too!

THE HOSPITALITY CUPBOARD

I recommend keeping a space for a bit of something to offer when an opportunity for welcome suddenly arises. I've come to call mine "The Hospitality Cupboard." It is amazing how a simple visit with a human is never simple. It's a privilege to share my space, and having a bit to offer honors the moment and affirms our shared incarnate experience of the world.

Humans are precious and welcome, whether they are here for a long stay, a Wednesday night Signpost Inn Evening, or dropping by as they pass through town on their way to the mountains. I'm invited to be in the presence of immortal beings who drink tea and like a little bit of something to eat, please.

To that end, I have little things on hand for guests. There are times for grand feasts, times for elaborate spreads, but the beauty of daily welcome is its simplicity and repetition. It's a pattern: candle, tea, platter, a bit of this and that. And when they visit again or another precious soul drops by: candle, tea, platter, a bit of this and that.

My kids have described it as magic: flamelight on mugs and a still-life of chocolate and walnuts. Like it appeared out of nowhere! And these vignettes of human community, gathered around the fire, keeping soul and body together, do feel like magic. But it is simple to conjure.

Keep a hospitality cupboard stocked with non-perishables and a corner dedicated to tea and an instant kettle. I have a bag of Ghiradelli 60% chocolate chips, walnuts, almonds, raisins, maybe dried coconut, dates, or figs if they're on sale. It doesn't have to be much or in great quantity. A plate of these, in sweet little piles is a beautiful, repeated pattern—always available, always with the same message: we're all human travelers here; we need a little sustenance; let's gather.

It seemed too simple at first, too "not enough," but if the welcome itself is truly enough, then the hospitality cupboard becomes a kind of sacristy, holding the physical elements that bring the spiritual truths to the literal table. We are simply visiting; we are also partaking.

Simple patterns repeated become beautiful, even culture-defining. Picture the Greek key design that frames pictures on pottery (also called "the meander"; isn't that wonderful?). It is the simplest possible element strung together over and over and over, but one quick glance cries out "Classical Greece!" and all the richness that comes with that. What a privilege that providing a simple consumable from the hospitality cupboard and receiving from it are the motif that repeated becomes the Christian life, beauty, welcome. Candle, tea, platter, a bit of this and that.

Maybe it's delightful for you to make something? It's true that there are few things as transporting as the smell of bread coming out of the oven. Maybe try this?

THE BREAD

So, this cracks me up. I am not an inexperienced baker or cook. I have lots of things I like to make for people, but in our home for a Wednesday Signpost Inn Evening, all anyone wants is what they all call "The Bread." It's a loosely-stretched focaccia flatbread the full size of a cookie sheet, sprinkled with salt and served hot for people to tear and dip in oil. I set this to rise at 6 pm so that at 7 or so, when our first guests are arriving, two large fresh trays are coming out of the oven, slid onto big wooden boards, and set on the table with garlic and herb dipping oil. I mean, it's good, but it's super basic. But really that's what I've been saying all along about incarnate grace, right?

They all ask for the recipe, so here it is in all its "nothing could be easier" glory. Call for tips if you need help.

FOCACCIA

"The Bread":

1 scant tbs yeast

1 Tbs kosher salt

3 ½ cups warm (not hot!) water

3 Tbs olive oil

About 8 cups flour

Knead 10 minutes (I use a standing mixer with a dough hook attachment)

- Add flour early on if it's soupy.
- It should come together as a slightly stiff dough and knead out to a very soft dough.

Turn over in an oiled bowl, cover with plastic wrap or a damp cloth, set to rise at least 1 hour, 90 minutes is better.

Preheat oven to 420 F.

Oil two cookie sheets generously, divide dough in two and gently hold up each half and let it stretch out, so you don't lose all the bubbles.

Lay the stretched-out dough on the sheet so it picks up some oil, then turn it over so it's oiled on both sides. It's ok if it's very uneven, even with a hole or two.

Sprinkle with additional kosher salt (you could also use crushed fresh rosemary–very yummy).

Bake 12-13 minutes until the bottom is golden to toasty.

Dipping oil:

Dice or run through a garlic press: 3-4 cloves of garlic.

Sauté in med-high heated oil until toasty brown.

Take off the heat, add Italian herbs, salt, pepper and more oil to the warm pan.

Pour / scrape the dipping oil into a heat-safe bowl.

Tear, dip and share!

IT DOESN'T HAVE TO BE FOOD

But it doesn't have to be food! Eating and drinking are fundamental human activities, of course, and they can be a powerful though simple way to welcome a guest, but there are other consumables.

A "consumable" really means something to put our hand to, something for our senses to share, something fleeting—perhaps disposable—that is just for this moment. Imagine you have a friend who loves to draw. They love to sit and sketch and maybe chat a bit. You don't have to be an artist to invite them over to sit by the lake and draw for a while. Even if you're terrible at drawing, your friend will enjoy that you made the effort to create a welcoming space that suits them! And maybe a bit of a laugh at your stick figures is the incarnate grace of hospitality—sharing who you are and what you have with someone else. The consumable that brings purpose to this space is paper, charcoal, a pencil, whatever. It's a shared physical offering that says, "You are worth my paper, my pencils, my attention, my time." Your work of art might end up on the fridge or in the bin. It's ok; it was only for this moment, this sacred lasting expression of welcome.

There are lots of ways to provide a consumable. I'm a sucker for paint parties. As a guest, I feel so welcomed when my spot at the table is laid out with my little foam tray of paint, my blank canvas, my brushes. I'm not a great artist, but I love that we will all try our hand at this project, sharing this consumable during this time frame. I belong here, connecting to those around me, and here's the proof—bloops of paint, all the colors I need, pre-set on my little foam tray.

21
HOW TO HOSPITALITY: A LOOSELY-COMMITTED-TO ACTIVITY

Liv

All the elements of hospitality serve one goal: to create a space of incarnate grace for the dear humans. What we consume, how long we're together and where we meet, are means to this end. And so is what we choose to do. A loosely-committed-to activity gives shape to our time.

Freedom is everything. GRACE (God's Riches At Christ's Expense) has been poured on me freely by the Lord who purchased and won me and included me in his kingdom. My enemies (sin, death and the devil) are defeated, and I live unencumbered—free to be loved and to love. So there is no requirement in any of this. You don't have to give your utmost best; you don't have to prove your capabilities or worth by what activity shapes your time with someone.

Here's a practical peek at my thought-process when it comes to choosing an activity:

"This person has asked for time to talk about something sensitive. We're meeting at 10 am on Saturday for two hours, and the weather is nice.

I need something private and quiet but open so they don't feel confined, something where we're not right across from each other in case they need a minute to process an emotion. They're pretty spry. Aha! Walking by the river where there are spots to get down to the edge and sit on rocks away from the main path."

or

"This person wants to be my friend, and I haven't been able to welcome them to my new apartment yet. I know they like challenging their baking skills, and there's that event coming up that we both intended to bake for anyway. Aha! I'll invite her to my new place to try out making those macarons we've all been nervous to try!"

or

"This person has been part of my support system in this community, but now I'm moving away. Pizza and a couple hours packing my house up into boxes. That's perfect."

See, the vulnerability of sharing who I am and what I have creates an honest, trusting atmosphere where I am free to connect. Free to give and free to receive love. Our activity can be almost anything, *including allowing a friend to help me pack*! What I have to share in that scenario is my need. How many people do we share our needs with? I would guess not many.

Why "loosely-committed-to"? Because it's not about me being good at doing stuff, and it's not about the activity. It's about the value of the people. If circumstances shift, the time is not "ruined" or "wasted." Take the baking example: we get together, assemble everything and go to preheat the oven. And the oven won't turn on. Boo. First order of business: laugh. That's life. The other elements of this beautiful moment of hospitality are intact: a guest, a space, a time frame, a consumable (even a glass of water). Don't give up! Set a new time for the baking if you want, get a couple glasses of water, sit on the porch for a few minutes and then say your goodbyes, chuckling at uncooperative appliances. After your guest leaves, call the repair guy.

What was the goal of the visit anyway? Yes, it would be fun if you'd tackled your new skill and had the photos to prove it, but the point was growing the friendship—and nothing brings people closer together than disappointment. So it was a win!

Your activities will change sometimes. Let them. That tight-fisted attitude that values programs over people squeezes love out until there's only room for control, stress and obsession over self-image. But mercy thrives in chaos.

Think of the miracle of the loaves and fishes. The people couldn't pay attention to Jesus anymore because it was time to eat, and they didn't have anything. He didn't roll his eyes and complain about how weak people are. He didn't freak out that his sermon wasn't done, and he had lost his audience. He saw that they didn't need to hear right now; they needed to eat. "You open your hand and satisfy the desires of every living thing." Out of his open hands came all they needed and more.

Hold activities (in fact ALL plans) with an open hand. The Lord does stuff on purpose to interrupt, reroute, and unravel our plans if he has something better in mind. He knows what he's doing. Trust his process.

22

BOUNDARIES

Liv

A strong warning: if we are to leap, trusting the Lord's kindness and provision, into a lifestyle of connecting with those around us, we need to be aware that we live in a fallen world, among sinful people (ourselves included). It is not safe to throw open the doors of your home and broadcast that you and your family are now—permanently and without boundaries—available to all comers.

Plans fail when we forget to take into account fallen, limited human nature. You must consider your safety, and your children's safety. Yes, God will provide so we need not fear being generous, but we must be wise with fallen human nature. Please keep in mind that Signpost Inn Ministries is not preaching a gospel of instant communal utopia. The gospel does not necessarily come with a house key.

We have been in ministry for over 20 years of person-to-person conversation and incarnate welcome, so I speak from real success and failure. We have met many people, and many kinds of people. We have made the mistake of assuming too much good from some people, and we have offered welcome to others without firm enough boundaries. I know now to operate by Jesus' rules, not my own. In his love and grace and in Christian freedom, hospitality becomes human-sized, human-shaped, human-proportioned. Incarnate. I am not God. I am only human. And he does not require me to save the world.

THE FIVE ELEMENTS

Reference the five elements of our framework "for scale." We little humans do little things. God makes them great or keeps them small according to his will. But we have short days, little stomachs, and brief attention spans. Hospitality is human-sized. You share what you have and who you are.

For those who try to do everything: If you have a fever, you cannot offer to babysit. If your bank account is empty, you cannot give $1,000 to the best cause on earth. Your day is 24 hours long. You do not have 26 to give.

For those who are afraid even to start: You do not need to open a bed-and-breakfast or host parties all the time! I am not joking: set a very, very small goal. How many times have you been out to coffee with someone from your church, school or work in the past year? No times? That's fine! This year, shoot for once. The welcome is so big, so life-giving! The impact of incarnate love in the world is that powerful.

IT'S ALL A GIFT

You are safe and free. The Lord is pleased with you. This is the result of living in the reality of the gospel. The eyes of faith see that every bit of what we've been given is a gift. We were bought by him, lock stock and barrel, and then he gave everything to us as a free gift, to enjoy and to use, to delight in, and to serve those around us. "Everything was made by him and for him." My home, husband, children, belongings—everything is his. And it's all mine, within reason.

"Within reason" doesn't take the gift back or lessen it. Imagine you're given a big jar of fancy hot cocoa mix for Christmas. Your 5-year-old comes up to you with her new mug, eyes alight, and says, "Can I have some cocoa!?" It is *your* cocoa mix, no doubt. But it would be ugly to snap at your 5-year-old, "No! Mommy gets ALL of this!" The delight of delighting your little one is part of the gift! You have cocoa to share!

And here is a reasonable boundary: share your gifts, and delight in the gift and the sharing. Should Mom get *no* cocoa? Of course not! It was a gift given to you, and you (just like Jesus) love to enjoy tasty things. Certainly enjoy it yourself along with them! It's good for them to see you loving things. It's how they learn to love!

The Lord will provide for all your needs. You will not

be forgotten. You are cared for and free to share your abundance. Your home belongs to you, within reason, and can be open to bless others, within reason. Which is to say that you are free to limit others' access to who you are and what you have. Just like a time frame, good boundaries are a mercy to both host and guest and prevent bitterness.

Here's what happens without boundaries:

A dear friend of ours grew up in a ministry home which prioritized generosity *without boundaries*. She tells the story of coming to the communal dinner table one evening and feeling pressured not to mention that a client has appeared at the table wearing her own shirt, taken out of her drawer without her knowledge, meaning that this client had wandered into the family quarters, opened her bedroom door, rooted through her things and chosen to wear her shirt to dinner, never mentioning it to her—certainly not asking permission. You can bet this brought bitterness to my young friend's heart.

Because of her parents' commitment to limitless generosity, my friend was compelled to give up any claim to private property. Which taught her that sharing could be dangerous. Share as you are able without bitterness, but, having mercy on your limitations and your heart, don't share if you find that you can't—for whatever reason. (And certainly don't share what isn't yours to give!)

Another example—this one from our family's experience of failure to set boundaries.

We had just escaped a dangerous living situation when

we worked for a ministry that was headquartered in Nowhere, Texas (not a real town, I don't think… or maybe it is…). We literally fled and found ourselves temporarily "homeless," or at least "between living situations."

We were led to Cañon City and a beautiful little rental house with a stunning view of mountains and valleys. We were so overwhelmed with God's generosity that we immediately offered a young man, whom we had known as a high school student, a portion of our gift and invited him to stay in the guest room while he figured out his next steps into the adult world.

The boundary problem? We set no clear expectations of his helpfulness in the home, his requirement to get a job, or a time limit on his stay. This very quickly led to bitterness for which I felt guilty, which led to more bitterness… And this poor clueless fellow continued to putter through our home as we were in a time of difficult transition. It ended badly.

With reasonable boundaries in place—rules, expectations, time limits—it might have been a great way to share God's bounty, but as it was, we were little help to this guy.

Sharing what I have (God's amazing bounty) and who I am (a totally free and beloved child of God) is best done in reasonable, human-sized proportion. I am not God; I cannot solve another's life by sacrificing myself (and my family). Have mercy, and set boundaries within your limited, human capacity.

CHILD SAFETY

Does your Spidey-sense tingle around some people, telling you they are not safe? Do you dismiss it, condemning yourself as judgmental, ungenerous, or oversensitive? In brief, maybe you're wrong about their untrustworthiness, but please listen to that sense. You must be kind and polite, explaining everything in the kindest way to yourself, but you are not required to trust anyone when it might put someone else in harm's way. Do not accuse anyone of anything until you have good reason, and never gossip about them. Gossip is the most powerful poison in the world and the death of hospitality. But do listen to your instincts.

Briefly: if that person even *seems* creepy, be respectful, but do not send your child over for a sleepover. And you are not required to extend hospitality to someone who seems unsafe. You are free to set limits on whom you host. "I guess it's ok" is not safe enough for your family.

Why the sudden alarmist tone? Don't I stand for freedom and release of control? It's because humans, as marvelously precious as they may be, are broken, and that makes every sinner at least a tiny bit dangerous.

There are people I trust, with whom I am happy to leave my kids, but even then it is on me to teach my children safety and personal boundaries. You must instill (as chill and low-emotion as you can), from three years old, bodily boundaries and a culture of open, calm communication between you and your children. Calm. Safe. Normal. You will create trust with your kids the more they know that you will not explode when you hear them say something scary. So you must be available to them to chat about whatever they're interested in (Zelda in our house … always Zelda…) for as long as you can reasonably take it, to establish that they really can bring anything at all to you.

Open communication saves families, even if harm is done. The Lord can use even the harm for amazing things. Your kids' lives are in his brilliant, wise, powerful, and tender hands.

PEOPLE AND PROPERTY SAFETY

Using good sense, we open our home on Wednesday nights from 7-10 pm for hospitality, but not our *whole* home. The upstairs and lower level are not available to guests. The open line-of-sight main floor and the fire pit out back are free and welcoming. This removes worry and communicates to everyone that our eyes are open. We hope for the best and prepare for the worst. Innocent as doves, wise as serpents.

Although I hold my possessions with an open hand, I don't have to tempt anyone by leaving money or jewelry lying about, or anything so valuable that my weak heart would have a hard time seeing it break or disappear. Remove opportunity for bitterness before it arises, and then of course, pray for help with your bitterness when it does… again, we are not immune from selfish responses.

Although our home is open, we do not post on Facebook that anyone in Cañon City may wander into our home.

We invite people, who invite people. In other words, the boundary is a purpose to the evening—anyone at all who is looking for what we have to offer is welcome. And what I have to offer is a safe, fun and wholesome atmosphere for a relatively tame time of hospitality and conversation. If that's what you want, you're welcome. But if you're looking for a loud, drunken brawl, try somewhere else.

Setting these boundaries creates the space we all need to be at ease, confident that we belong, reasonably certain that we are safe. It is all for mercy.

ST. STEPHEN

But, let's face it, maybe the Lord will require your total abandonment and giving of self. Ask St. Stephen. American Christians don't like to mention it, but the time is drawing nearer in this country when we will not only be, as we are now, ridiculed and dismissed, but stripped of property or even physically martyred. We live in an unusual time of peace. But you might be called to missions elsewhere or to suffering here, and you are free to risk the life God has redeemed and gifted to you in his service or in the service of others—an intense instance of sharing who you are and what you have.

You see? Hospitality is serious business, with its roots in Christ's sacrificial love and its expression in our limited, incarnate selves. We come to experience the God of Cana—the one who sees and fulfills our need for belonging, for delight, for joy—through another person first. And, though still surrounded by a world that has forgotten how to be human, we learn to be human as he is human: made to give and receive incarnate love.

23

GUESTING

Liv

So much about hosting! What about guest-ing!? My friend Catherine grew wide-eyed as I described how we extend hospitality at Signpost Inn retreats, Wednesday nights, and in impromptu community dinners. She felt inadequate and intimidated. "I don't host people. I don't cook, and I have no idea how to set a table. I love getting together with people, but I'd much rather it was at someone else's house. Does that make me a bad person? Do I need to host???"

No, of course not! If everyone were a host, who would fill the tables? Hospitality is a value we all share. We want it to happen in our communities, so we support its existence, yes, by hosting, but also by guesting!

Revealing a big secret about me: I'm scared to death of attending events. Even little ones. Because my pride tempts me to Be Awesome, it is easier for me to host than to show up as a guest! The same way it's easier to love than to accept love.

I believe in scruffy hospitality, and I'm comfortable putting on big to-dos, so I can host comfortably—trusting that the welcome is enough. What I've offered is enough. But underneath… I still don't believe that I'm enough, and that makes guest-ing agony. Receiving an invitation sends me into a death-spiral of shame and uncertainty. "They're inviting me to be polite." "I'm too old for this group of young moms. They probably just feel bad for me." "I don't know most of these people; what do I have to offer them?" "If I'm just a guest, I can't help."

It seems to me there are lots of reasons to fear being a guest, so when Catherine shared her fear of hosting but not of guest-ing I stood in awe and chose to write this section to honor her bravery and my fear.

When you guest (Yes, I'm verbing the noun. "Guesting" is more than "attending." It is assuming the role of "receiver of grace"—the role to which every Christian is called!) You bring only yourself. You are enough, and you are responding to the call of welcome. What is this other than the very heart of the Bride of Christ? He calls, "Come away, my love!" and our heart's cry is, "Yes, Lord! Love me!" Amazing! I highly honor every heart that can respond easily to an invitation with "Yay! They want me!" Oh, to believe the welcome like that—without resistance.

If that's you, take a minute to thank God for the gift of "guesting with ease." I honor and admire you. But if you're like me, these very recent scenarios might feel familiar:

1) The dearest of friends, who have walked through the Valley of the Shadow of Death with us, texted last night offering a last-minute dinner at their house for us and four of our kids. Well, I had been working at many tasks all day and was just flopping down to some TV-show quantity time with my daughters and thought, "Oh man, I love Faith and Jacob, and I can't wait to meet their foster baby, but there will be another night…" and I turned down the invite. Then a little voice said two things, "It's only 4:30. You have plenty of evening left," and "Um, so do we support hospitality in the community or not?" So I texted again. We finished our show, hopped into the car, and—as guests—had an absolutely fantastic evening of food, a hilarious game, and some much-needed baby snuggles. We left remembering that we have family in town, that Jesus cares for us through a brother and sister in him.

2) A group of young women included me in their text thread about a Sunday evening snack-and-game time. My brain turned to moosh with all the usual doubts. These are all people I love and have had to my house many times, but as a guest, I had to hold with both hands to my principle that I support hospitality in the community—that it is life and incarnate grace—in order to accept the invite, step out my door, and show up. And, of course, we had a lovely

time with good laughs and the magic of welcome doing its thing. A piece of my heart is softer for going.

My heart is softer because it had been allowed to do what it is made for—to receive love. Remember the Lord's first miracle? "Jesus and his disciples were invited to a wedding…." When you respond freely to an invitation, you are doing what Jesus did and what we are made for! He showed his glory in this first miracle: He showed us how to attend a wedding, and he made that good party better—creating and multiplying the best wine so that every guest's heart was full and their joy complete. As John would say later, recognizing Jesus when he overloaded the empty nets with miraculous fish, "That's so the Lord."

When you accept an invitation from a believer, you are walking into a taste of the Wedding at Cana. A party where Jesus sits next to you in your awkwardness and smiles at your joy. Where he laughs at your dumb jokes and listens to your anecdotes. He is at ease with you. You can be at ease, too.

The Wedding at Cana itself was just a foretaste of the Feast to come! Jesus invites the Church (all of God's people everywhere— and everywhen) to receive free grace. In the end, we are all wedding guests, dressed in Jesus' righteousness, feasting with him—belonging at the table. We are made for guesting!

So I guess it shouldn't surprise me that some of you are not afraid of guesting—to some it feels as natural as it is. Maybe you even have the instinct that you are enough, which you are! I am so grateful for you! It takes all of us to create that foretaste of the Feast to come. We're made to be supportive of and involved in hospitality. And it's possible and healthy for both those who fear guesting to guest and for those who fear hosting to host. Eventually, you find yourself in one role or the other.

The Body of Christ is made up by many different members. We create hospitable spaces so differently! My friend Faith's welcome usually includes a meal, chatting, a game, and lots of laughter. Someone else's space might look very different but offer the same incarnate grace. So Catherine hates cooking (and even sitting still) but she comes alive organizing hiking groups, encouraging people on the trail, and sitting with them at the summit, welcoming them into this space to share what she has and who she is. She can bring Jesus' love and inclusion to some people that I can't reach. Literally. Because they're on top of a fourteen-thousand-foot mountain.

24

I NEEDED TO SEE IT FIRST

Liv

I hope these chapters have been practical encouragement that you can "do" hospitality on your own. But I only know what I know because I experienced it from other people. If you don't feel ready to create a hospitable space yourself, take up invitations to dinner or a hosted event. Take every opportunity to be a guest. Hospitality spreads as soon as we see how it's done. It speaks directly to our human heart; we recognize it, and we want to repeat it. But we need to see it first.

Let me show you what I mean by sharing some of my own experience with you. Look for the five elements of hospitality I laid out earlier: a person, a space, a time frame, a consumable, a loosely-committed-to activity. Lives arranged by and for hospitality. And remember, hospitality takes different forms and speaks to each of us differently. This is just what I saw.

We were a noisy, scrappy gang of Christmas carolers, making the rounds of the college town our freshman year, being sure to stop at the Whalens' since Janet, we were told, would probably "have something nice for us." We expected a welcome, blithely invaded her home, and she served hot cider from a giant pot on the kitchen stove. I pitched in, helping to ladle cider into mugs, laughing with everyone else about the Michigan cold and taking in the happy evening. Janet laughs with her whole self. She laughs at herself, at her funny kids (there are, I think, eleven now). She laughs at youth, at age, at absurdity. And that evening of openness, generosity, delight, acceptance sealed something that I had always known, but hadn't put into a category yet: hospitality is life. And I learned it from Janet.

Christy Kalthoff, also a professor's wife, wove the same magic. Their home was quieter, removed from town on a few wooded acres. They had chickens, a goat, two turkeys, four tall, strong children (five now) and a potato bin in the cellar. I mention the potato bin because it was another of those confirming elements for me. Christy thought ahead, bought a share of a farmer's potatoes and stored them in the cool cellar so she'd always have enough to give. And every dinner to which I was invited was plentiful and accompanied by meaty conversation. Any old evening, there was a Home there. It was life. And I learned it from Christy.

My own mother is not naturally social. It is draining for her to have evenings full of people or deep, difficult conversation with a relative stranger, but her big yearly gesture of hospitable magic is the most powerful in my life. She began the tradition of a midnight Easter Feast in the home. Bursting out at midnight with music and light after the darkness of a long, cold, hungry Lent, Easter Feast began with a blast on the shofar (yes, the curly ram's horn thing) and then a crowd of our friends joined us for food, drink and song to celebrate the resurrection. This is life, let me tell you. I, my sisters, and now others, keep this tradition, and it has been, it is not too much to say, transformative for those who have experienced it. It is life. And we learned it from my mother.

Hospitality is the opening of everything that is good about what you have and what you are to those around you. A hospitable life is an honest life, and as you give what you really are, you make your own life better, so that you have more to share, which makes your life better, so that you have more to share, which makes your life better, so that you have more to share … you see where I'm going here.

You can see in the three above examples that hospitality weaves a spell. It's not fake, but it is theatrical. It requires a set, some props and a few lines. Humans are incarnate; we live in our bodies and among objects. We eat and drink and breathe and all the rest. Although hospitality is done by a person, the physical environment itself speaks powerfully. It teaches and demonstrates truths. Janet's kitchen wanted the students to be in it. The smell of cider told us that. The mugs higgledy-piggledy on the counter told us there was enough for all and that we were not to stand on ceremony. "Come on in," said the kitchen light. "Relax," said the chairs pulled away from the table. This environment welcomed us in proportion to the welcome of our hosts.

The environment literally taught us. It was still Advent, the run-up to Christmas, and Janet's kids had made paper Advent wreathes and pinned them to the kitchen wall. This family watched time go by, observed and celebrated the feasts and fasts of the church year. Janet made pretzels during Advent, which symbolize praying arms. We had been caroling, and this home, these people, clearly supported us in that. More than supported, they enjoyed our joy.

A prayer card and a candle on her cluttered desk spoke to her own, private devotion in the midst of her busy life. I learned by seeing that card that a busy mother, wife, American woman, was still a person, a single soul in front of God. She had a hidden life. Her candle taught me to want one too. I wanted to live like that.

Christy's home in a clearing in the woods, with piles of firewood, pens of animals to be fed and cared for, and a large yard to be raked and mowed all spoke of the richness of labor. I worked with Christy in that yard, raking and hauling tarps of debris to the edge of the wood, when she was eight months pregnant. She was so strong, indomitable, but she allowed me to help her. Her hospitality welcomed my effort. The extra gloves, ready on the porch, told me I was good enough to help. In fact, my helpfulness was valuable. I wanted that to be part of my life.

Inside Christy's home, where many people have walls, the Kalthoffs had bookshelves. Mark's study was central in the house and above it was a loft surrounded by the children's books and many others. Christy kept these spaces clear and usable. She was a powerhouse of a woman and a sharp, clear thinker. I remember learning more from Mark and Christy at their table than in Mark's classroom. What I learned in class was so valuable, but I have carried into my own life far more daily wisdom that I learned at that table. Maybe sometimes to Christy it was "one more student meal," but to me it was a pattern for the rest of my life. Not "how to be perfect." I knew they weren't. But "how to welcome them in." Hospitality. Life.

The set and props of my mother's Easter Feast preached a depth charge of truth and formed how I live. I think I can just describe it, and you'll hear what I mean. We observed Lent for forty days, more or less. More prayer, fewer sweet treats, and awareness of the season. The anticipation of the feast grew as Lent passed. And then Easter—Easter was the center of our universe.

I am going to take the time to paint this picture for you, using an excerpt from another writing project. Keep in mind, as I do, the power of objects, of meeting with acceptance and belonging in a physical space by hospitality, to make a message present and powerful, to give life.

> The sanctuary was entirely dark at the end of the Tenebrae service on Good Friday—the service of the

shadows. A pair of beeswax tapers burned on the altar as the final words of Christ rang out into the silence, "It is finished." An acolyte rises from his knees and puts out one of the weak flames with the bell of the long brass snuffer (*emunctorium*, I have heard it was called, though we never used the term). All eyes are on the final flame, a spark in this vast space. I will it to burn on, not to waver, not to quake. "Father! Into your hands I commend my spirit." A Father who was not listening. Don't put it out. God, let the last one stay lit. It's so dark in here. But the acolyte rises, a black shape of robes against the pool of yellow light, extends the brass bell on its long handle like a stiff tentacle, and it descends upon the final taper, suffocating it and leaving us alone in total darkness. Some weep, all are sober, all recall His every word as we stand and file silently back toward the narthex and into the dim and thinly street-lamp-lit night. "Father, forgive them. They don't know what they're doing." "I'm thirsty." "Eloi! Eloi! Lama sabacthani?" I often cried in my bed on Good Friday, thinking of Him dying slowly, intentionally, with all His wits about Him.

Holy Saturday was for cleansing. We turned the heat off, threw open every door and window. The smell of dust on the metal screens being blown inward by cold, moist New England spring air as I crank open my bedroom window is the smell of anticipation, preparation, hard work and hunger.

We fasted on Holy Saturday, water only. Coffee for the grown-ups—every adult in my family drank strong, black coffee all day. Little kids were given bread and milk, but the unspoken challenge was to graduate to a full fast and declare yourself an adult. And once there, you wouldn't go back, any more than you would return to diapers. "Did Emmy fast today?" "No, she's still on bread and milk." "I'm *growing*!"

Windows open, we blared show tunes, filled pails with warm suds and rags made from Pop's old undershirts and our old cloth diapers, and washed everything. Until I was in college, my dad smoked a corncob pipe, pacing the hall as he wrote sermons in his head, and the tar clung to the white walls in a yellow gradation from ceiling downward. The clean white arc that my soapy rag made through the grime was satisfying enough to make me want to clean for hours. And we really did.

When Janna put on the soundtrack to 'Me and My Girl,' we all belted the numbers as we cleaned, more or less in good spirits until the hunger wore us down.

When the walls were done and all the linens washed, the wooden furniture oiled and the Persian-style area rugs taken up for the season, we washed and waxed the wood floors. Even though we were very hungry, and the work was physically tiring, it was a very great pleasure for all the senses to kneel on the clean, dry dull boards of the floor and rub in bowling alley wax with rags, conditioning, darkening, reviving the wood. And then we buffed it.

We had a buffing machine, with thick, round felt pads on the bottom for the large, main areas, but we always finished the buffing with cloth diapers tied thickly around our feet. Miriam and I skated around the floor, rubbing any dull spots to shining splendor. And the smell: soap, lemon, fresh earth, the yeast of babka and kulich developing richly with vanilla and orange rind, vinegar, bacon for a marvelous pickled cabbage dish I later dubbed "Moscow kapusta." Raisins, citron and sugar for the hot crossed buns. You can live on these smells for a day without eating.

We learned anticipation. At gatherings of friends and festive dinners, my dad always smiled, sighed, and thanked God for "this foretaste of the feast to come." I didn't know then that I was practicing for the rest of my life. And I didn't know he was quoting the eucharistic liturgy. Holy Saturday is where we live our human lives. God seems to have left us without restoring what we thought He'd restore. We yearn. We all yearn. It is the fundamental truth in man's heart, from Gilgamesh to Siddhartha. The gnawing hunger while we work in preparation for we know not what, will be satisfied. But not yet. We are fasting, and we can do it more or less cheerfully, more or less busy along the way, making our life beautiful and fragrant.

We went to bed exhausted, and I haven't described all the cooking, baking and errand running involved before evening fell. I always thought I wouldn't sleep, like the night before Christmas. Miriam and I were so hungry and proud of ourselves for keeping the fast that we had already chosen what we'd break it with at midnight, sometimes it was already hidden beneath our pillows—a chocolate egg, a piece of bread, always forgotten when midnight finally came.

Janna stayed up with my parents finishing the production. Every potted lily, hyacinth and tulip that would later bedeck the sanctuary had been carried up through the frosty night from the church to the parsonage, not too early, or they'd wilt in the heat of the house warmed with baking breads. The fragrant blooms in their linen-wrapped pots sprang from any spot left between the sweet Russian breads, pickled things, boiled sausage, steaming white potatoes, cold butter shaved into curls by one lucky daughter, cabbage with bacon, kvass, preserves, rye bread, cheap caviar, sour cream, and a strewing of Jordan almonds and Cadbury mini eggs, and all of it served in crystal or on glowing silver trays and platters newly polished by one unlucky daughter, and all of that on crisp and creamy linen—ironed wet so that its smoothness shone.

All of these waited in the dark. It wasn't time yet. The usual guests pulled up quietly just before midnight. They found their way up the driveway over the little ridges of the remaining icy snow, between rows of flickering candles we'd set in glass jars to lead them to our basement door. Twelve or so waited downstairs in the dark—the signal hadn't come yet.

Then midnight—no more could be readied—the time was come. We had a ram's horn, and this was the time to use it. It called out, hollow, pure and distant in mounting harmonics and then the music played loud, and the candles were lit, and the friends charged up the basement stairs, and my father laughed aloud.

Miriam and I woke to music and my father's cry of "Christ is risen!" as he threw open our bedroom door. Shaking, we replied "He is risen indeed!" and joined the party.

The pleasures of the Feast were of every kind. My father raised a glass of ice-cold vodka and toasted his throaty, "To the King!" We downed the freezing liquid fire and willed to keep it in our empty stomachs as Pop sighed and prayed over the food we were craving.

I found my place in the candlelight, glowing with vodka and spiritual release. My people were around me; my God had conquered death; the best of foods lay before me, and I ate. And when the ache of my heart and my empty belly were satisfied, I breathed and sat back in my chair and looked around the table and listened to the talk.

"A great babka, Mom. One for the books."

"Thank you. I got so nervous when the top was really overflowing the pan and getting so dark. I had to put foil over it so it wouldn't burn."

"No, it turned out great."

"What's this one?"

"Oh, that's poppyseed."

"You know, you can make kvass out of almost anything."

"Fruit usually, though, right?"

"Best pickled eggs ever."

"Definitely, and did you use a thicker bacon in the sour cabbage?"

The murmur and pleasant observations didn't ever seem to stop, and I loved watching their faces. Across the table in the candlelight, you and I smiled and pretended to understand all the grownups talked about. This glittering table was the point of reconnection as we grew and our lives changed.

Do I need to explain how powerful those nights were? Every last physical detail spoke joy, pleasure, richness, peace, satisfaction, triumph and unity, The Marriage Feast of the Lamb, which is the point of Jesus' mission. Our firm anticipation of our own bodily resurrection from the dead acted out by eating sweet, filled breads and caviar. And it was at a table, where there were chairs for everyone.

...

This example is a pinnacle of hospitality, a grand production. But powerful hospitality doesn't need a crowd. You don't need a big family, full table or silver serving platters. The same welcome, with the same power, exists between two people, when one gives and another receives. This back-and-forth, this conversation, is the stuff of life. And life can be small; it can be messy; it can certainly be flawed.

Bringing all of who you are means not hiding the rough edges, not pretending any kind of absolute control over self or situation. Those who have taught me hospitality the most beautifully have done it the most helter-skelter. The Whalens used the line I now use about my own family, "The train keeps rolling, but if you can jump on board, you're more than welcome!"

I needed to see it first. My invitation to you is to see it

too. Keep your eyes open. Be receptive to the love and welcome, the presence of God, in other people first. Allow yourself to connect, however awkwardly. Then go, make your own oases. Find and welcome those other froggy (or hawky!) friends for the sake of Jesus, for the sake of what he made us to be, for the sake of being human.

ABOUT SIGNPOST INN MINISTRIES

We created Signpost Inn Ministries in 2020 for the disconnected, the wanderer, the one who feels that God is far away, the one who aches for reconnection. And because we all feel that at one time or another, Signpost Inn is for all of us. Our mission is to strengthen your relationship with Jesus and walk compassionately with you on life's journey.

I (Liv) feel the need for those "Beavers' Dam" moments, a restful pause on the journey, to be welcomed body and soul, and to be reminded what the journey is for. My home has welcomed many travelers in Jesus' name, including our own five children. I have experienced and believe deeply in the power of welcoming love expressed through the physical—the freedom to find and express joy one human to another, through food, drink, art, music—the crucial things.

I (Brandon) love wide-open spaces, long conversations about big ideas, and living in the tension of paradox. I earned a bachelor's in philosophy from Hillsdale College, and a master's in historical theology from Concordia Seminary, St. Louis. I am a ministry veteran, having served and led in various capacities for more than 25 years, but always focused on connecting people more deeply with Jesus. I completed my official training as a spiritual director early in 2023, but have been offering spiritual direction (without knowing it) for much longer. Spiritual direction facilitates and encourages people's experience with God. I love to help people discern God's invitations, corrections, and challenges, and to support them as they take any "leaps of faith" God may ask of them.

Together, whether on the road with college staff, on an evening with students in our home, or while catching up with the same people years later as their lives and questions changed, we have always created spaces of welcome for listening, conversation, soul struggle and rest, and refreshment for soul and body.

When it came time to follow Jesus into the creation of Signpost Inn Ministries, it was the obvious move to combine our strengths and work together—welcoming the traveler and offering a moment of rest to listen for the Lord and direct people's attention to his loving presence and action in their lives.

HÅKENFRØGG

Combining our strengths helped us to learn about each other … which brings us to Hawk and Frog. We married in 2002, and it's no secret to us that we are very different from one another. It has been helpful to lean into it. It didn't take long to settle on the helpful metaphor: Brandon is a Hawk. Liv is a Frog.

Hawk's far-seeing, big-picture, brightly-illuminated solo flights describe Brandon's way of living precisely. He loves freedom and perspective, and he really hates getting his "feathers drippy." His path of growth has been into community with others, connecting his brain to his body, learning to ride the updraft of God's love rather than relying on the power of his correct knowledge or strong wings.

Frog's path of growth has been to trust the loving provision of God when there is no swamp to be found. Frog grew up close to the earth, no more than a croak's distance from many froggy relatives. She lives in details, poetically connecting immediate sensations to big ideas. Built for cool, shady, squishy, comfortable, green surroundings, Frog is driven by instinct to find or create oases however she can wherever her travels may take her and to gather any of God's creatures in need of rest.

Hawk and Frog (or in fake Norwegian "Håkenfrøgg") have created an unlikely alliance and a home full of children trying to figure out what they are! With mercy on and appreciation for God's differing designs for everyone, we live as a family and community receiving our daily bread and relying on the Lord who guards our ways and is leading us to our real home. In the meantime, we are not home yet.

www.signpostinn.org

Our Ministries:

Spiritual direction: Confidential, one-on-one sessions, online or in person. Strengthen your relationship with God and deepen your intimacy with him.

Soul-nourishing retreats: Peace for your soul and new direction for your spiritual journey. Come experience the incarnate grace of hospitality.

Faith-sustaining resources: Support for you along life's winding way. Engage with our podcast, events, and weekly email.

www.ingramcontent.com/pod-product-compliance
Lightning Source LLC
Chambersburg PA
CBHW070532090426
42735CB00013B/2959